"In recent days, the word *transformation* has joined terms like apostolic, seeker-sensitive, and purpose-driven on the list of Christian buzzwords. Everybody, it seems, has something to say about the necessity or means of transforming a life, institution, or society.

"What makes Rhonda Hughey's book stand out from the crowd is her refreshing—and critical—emphasis on *Presence*. . . . She reasons that if we set out to entertain His Presence (as a primary motive), we will also have that which this Presence brings (a blessed bonus). It is a remarkably clutter-free approach.

"Although *Desperate For His Presence* is strewn with relationally-oriented subtleties, it is no collection of gooey sentimentality. It offers premises that are based on solid biblical research and illustrated with real-world case studies. Its conclusions are tough-minded practicality.

"Attracting and maintaining God's presence may not be complicated, but neither is it easy. If you want a reminder of what is required, read on. But if you are looking for spiritual cotton candy, or someone to give you good news about bad habits, this is decidedly *not* your ticket."

—George Otis, Jr.
Founder and president of The Sentinel Group, author of *Informed Intercession*

"In *Desperate for His Presence* Rhonda Hughey goes deep into the heart of God to remind His Bride—the church—of some foundational truths about her identity and purpose often obscured by our frantic, performance-driven culture. Rhonda presents a compelling case to the church to embrace the personal and corporate transformation necessary to effectively minister to communities, cities, and even nations. This is a book that will change lives, and a message that will empower the church to fulfill her purpose in God to bring transformation to cities and nations, and ultimately help witness the fulfillment of the Great Commission in our generation."

—Rev. Ed Silvoso
President of Harvest Evangelism, Inc. and author of *Anointed for Business*

"*Desperate for His Presence* is a book bringing fresh and unique revelation into God's burning heart to bring cities into their sovereign destiny and purposes through the grace on His church.

"This book will stir you, challenge you, and invite you into a life-changing encounter with God both for you and your community. You will be inspired to pray with renewed faith and vision that our cities would become places of refuge as the presence of God dwells in fullness in the midst of a unified church.

"Rhonda's years of experience in this area of the kingdom and her global perspective, genuine prophetic insights and fiery devotion to Jesus make this book a hope-filled prophetic journey for hearts for the glorious habitation of God!"

—Mike Bickle
Director of the International House of
Prayer of Kansas City

"I have never met Rhonda Hughey, but when I perused the manuscript of *Desperate for His Presence* I was acutely aware of an enormous spiritual affinity and unity of heart over issues that for decades have been an integral part and emphasis of my life and teaching. My spirit strongly resonates with approval as I wholeheartedly endorse the truths of this powerful book."

—Joy Dawson
International Bible teacher and author

"It is one thing to theologically describe the importance of God's presence in our lives; it is quite another to truly be *desperate* for the reality of God. It is the desperate heart that God seeks, and this is the heart Rhonda Hughey offers. In so doing, she awakens us to the reality of what God offers to us in order that we might become truly desperate for more of Him."

—Francis Frangipane
Senior minister, River of Life Ministries,
author

RHONDA HUGHEY

# Desperate
## FOR HIS
## PRESENCE

GOD'S DESIGN

TO TRANSFORM

YOUR LIFE

AND YOUR

CITY

BETHANYHOUSE
MINNEAPOLIS, MINNESOTA

*Desperate for His Presence*
Copyright © 2004
Rhonda Hughey

Cover design by Greg Jackson (Arkansas)

Published by Bethany House Publishers
11400 Hampshire Avenue South
Bloomington, Minnesota 55438

Bethany House Publishers is a division of
Baker Publishing Group, Grand Rapids, Michigan.

Printed in the United States of America

ISBN-13:  978-0-7642-0007-6
ISBN-10:  0-7642-0007-0

**Library of Congress Cataloging-in-Publication Data**

Hughey, Rhonda.
    Desperate for His presence: God's design to transform your life and your city / by Rhonda Hughey
        p.   cm.
    ISBN 0-7642-0007-0
    1. City churches.  2. Revivals.  I. Title.

    BV637.H84    2004
    269'.2—dc22                                                        2004012005

# About the Author

RHONDA HUGHEY has served in city-wide ministry and the international prayer movement for a decade. She travels nationally and internationally, igniting faith and vision for prayer, revival, and transformation. Her desire is to see people restored by the love and power of Jesus and for His glory to be reflected through His church, resulting in the evangelization of the lost and transformation of the community.

Rhonda's ministry is characterized by an encouraging faith that comes from her personal experience with revival and transformation in the nations. Her journey has led her through many streams in the church, depositing in her a deep love for the diversity found in the bride of Christ and the fruitfulness that results from unifed partnership for Kingdom purposes.

Rhonda is the founder and director of Fusion Ministries, Inc. She also serves on the senior leadership team at the International House of Prayer in Kansas City. In addition, Rhonda partners with George Otis Jr. (The Sentinel Group) and John Dawson (YWAM) in transformation activities in cities and nations. Rhonda makes her home in Kansas City, Missouri.

# Acknowledgments

Thank you, Wes Adams! The fire of God in your life has been such an inspiration, and your friendship is a treasure to me. Thank you for your encouragement and insight that helped me articulate on paper what burns in my heart.

Special thanks to my mom, dad, and sister, Renae, my heroes and friends! Thank you for your love, patience, and encouragement. You have undergirded me in so many ways and provided such a foundation of love and joy in my life!

Thanks to the many friends who have walked with me through the process of writing this book. Thank you for your prayers and encouragement, and for believing the Lord with me for this project to be completed.

A big "thank-you" to our team and ministry partners at Fusion Ministries! What a gift from the Lord each of you are, what a joy to serve the Lord with you. Thank you for your hard work and dedication to see the Lord Jesus glorified in cities and nations.

A special thanks to those friends who have shared their stories—may the Lord be glorified through your testimony and ignite faith in the hearts of many others!

I also want to thank Kyle, Julie, Jeanne, and the rest of the team at Bethany House. What a great team you are to work with! I have been so impressed with your integrity, humility, and love for the Lord. Thank you for believing in this message and your desire to communicate it with excellence.

# Contents

*Desperate for His Presence* is a prophetic message addressing revival in the church and the transformation of our cities. As we face an increased challenge in influencing and championing the cause of Christ in cities and nations, this book will inspire you to consider core pursuits of God's kingdom: intimacy with Jesus, revival in His church, and His promise of transforming the cities and communities where we live.

Have you connected with God's heart and vision? Do you "hear what the Spirit is saying" to the church? This book is a bridge of hope in the midst of confusion and complacency, directing us not only back to God but also to one another.

Rhonda Hughey is a remarkable woman. She is one of that rare band of people who live in true service to us all in the body of Christ. Many believers learn about the big picture, follow trends, and talk about developments, but Rhonda is one of the few world Christians who has been a genuine catalyst for change.

Rhonda's passion and vision for what God longs to accomplish in our communities is contagious and will stir your heart to pray with vision and faith regarding your destiny and the destiny of your city.

In this book she has collected a treasure of wisdom from the city-reaching, nation-transforming movements around the world. However, Rhonda is more than a steward of knowledge. She is a woman of God worth knowing, an authentic leader.

She has used her perspective as a close associate of ministries such as Harvest Evangelism, Youth With A Mission, Promise Keepers, International House of Prayer, The Sentinel Group, and the International Reconciliation Coalition. She has been a contributing leader within these movements, not just an observer. In this book she is able to summarize the path to breakthrough that is being rediscovered in contemporary movements and to illustrate values and principles through stories gleaned from the cities where she is currently engaged. These contemporary reports make this book truly exciting!

An inspirational book is in some ways a long letter from a new friend, but a book never fully captures the pathos of a heroic and sacrificial life. Read between the lines and you will see Rhonda—a dedicated, humble servant of Jesus who has set aside every other priority in order to know God intimately and to experience His presence in the midst of a united, healed, effective church.

Her perspective is global, her teaching is deep, her insights are timely and prophetic. But most of all, her life is an inspiration. God will illuminate the path into your own future as you read these pages. This is the way to spiritual authority and the joy of a transformed world.

John Dawson
International Reconciliation Coalition
President, YWAM International

# THE INVITATION

We are living in unprecedented days in the history of the church! The Lord is moving in powerful ways, building His church and expanding His kingdom. Revival is impacting many cities and nations. Leaders are praying with anticipation that they might cross the threshold into genuine revival, leading to transformation of cities in the United States and the Western world. This is not a "trend" or the latest ministry strategy. We are beginning to see tangible evidence of God's intention to fulfill His promise in Scripture to restore and rebuild cities that are desolate.

By His own design, God has ordained seasons of revival throughout history to restore His church to simplicity, power, and effectiveness. God intends that His glory be manifested "in the church and in Christ Jesus throughout all generations forever and ever!" (Eph. 3:21 NIV). His will could not be more explicit. He desires that His glory be manifested in the church in every generation and in every culture. The world will see the glory of God only when Jesus Christ is clearly seen in the church—and through the church to the world (as Jesus prays in John 17).

Scripture promises that a mighty outpouring of God's glory is coming (Joel 2) that will include signs and wonders, a harvest of souls, and the Gospel being preached to the ends of the earth (Matthew 24:14). We have a responsibility as the people of God to cry out for His presence to fill our communities toward that end. The church is not meant to be a spectator on the sidelines; God is inviting us into full partnership with this end-of-the-age drama.

Are we ready for what God has in mind? Is the church prepared to walk out the reality of the promises God has made in His Word? Many would suggest that, although we are at a critical threshold of history, the church is not up to the challenge and unprecedented opportunity that is before us. The current condition of the church suggests that we have replaced the purity and simplicity of the gospel with sophisticated, entertaining activities that have left people inside and outside the community of faith questioning the reality of Jesus Christ and His life-changing power. Both leaders and laypeople in the Western church are questioning foundational doctrines of the Christian faith, leaning more and more toward humanistic ideologies in contrast to the moral and spiritual absolutes of Scripture and a biblical worldview.

A recent survey conducted by noted researcher George Barna reported that the large majority of Americans now contend that there is no absolute moral truth. More than two out of three adults, Christian and non-Christian alike, argue that truth is relative to the individual and circumstances.[1] Moral and ideological relativism, which has characterized Western universities for many decades, is now prevalent everywhere in our culture. Most alarming is the way this relativism is being embraced by much of the church, resulting in a new level of tolerance and comfort with sin, even when it blatantly contradicts the clear teaching of God's Word. The Western worldview has replaced the biblical worldview, and relativism now functions in partnership with the appearance of Christian "faith." As the faith of believers has become diluted, so the influence and relevance of the church has diminished in society. This disconnect of the church ultimately derives from a decline in knowing God; the lack of an intimate relationship with Jesus by believers has resulted in a loss of true identity, lack of spiritual authority, and a lack of awareness of the church's transforming purpose.

In response, the church as a whole seems determined to find the answer within herself, giving rise to endless agendas to solve the identified problems. We have been recycling religious programs and activities, hoping that somehow they will become effective the "next time." Desperate to appear "unique" in order to attract members, we have wandered further and further from the simple and powerful gospel of Jesus Christ. As a result, much of our religious activity has served as a numbing agent for believers rather than producing disciples for the kingdom. At this writing, there are ten million born-again believers who are unchurched.[2] Even believers are becoming bored and disillusioned!

The Western church is struggling with her identity, authority, and purpose. Understanding our true identity in Christ must occur before we can exercise spiritual authority and accomplish our God-given mission as an agent of change on the earth. We need a serious lifestyle change in the body of Christ, from a Westernized culture of Christianity to becoming radical disciples of Jesus. If we are conformed to His image, we can become the "fragrance of Christ among those who are being saved and among those who are perishing" (2 Cor. 2:15).

In a declining culture, the church cannot fully recover the presence of God in her midst apart from the catalyst of a true revival from heaven. We are living in an important hour of history! God is challenging the church's self-centered identity and shifting our mindsets and ineffective methodologies. He is inviting us to respond to one of the greatest challenges we have ever faced—to return to our first love and to step out of our compromised church culture into His kingdom!

In order to fulfill the purposes of God for our cities, we must hear what the Spirit is saying to the church and be obedient to His voice. Isaiah prophesied: "Pass through, pass through the gates! Prepare the way for the people. Build up, build up the highway! Remove the stones. Raise a banner for the nations" (Isa. 62:10 NIV). The Lord is issuing an invitation to His church to pass through a threshold into the reality of His kingdom. He is opening three "gates" or doorways before us.

The first door is the **Door of Intimacy**. Scripture contains two pictures of this door. The first is found in the Song of Solomon: "I sleep, but my heart is awake; it is the voice of my beloved! He knocks, saying, 'Open for me, my sister, my love, my dove, my perfect one'" (5:2). A second picture is found in the book of Revelation: "Behold, I stand at the door and knock. If anyone hears My voice and opens the door, I will come in to him and dine with him, and he with Me" (Rev. 3:20). Jesus is knocking at the door of His church, longing for fellowship and intimacy with His beloved. This door must be opened before the church can become like Jesus. We can only become what we are beholding in prayer and intimate fellowship. By fixing our gaze on Him, we can be transformed into His image, from glory to glory.

The second door is a **Door of Hope**. In Hosea we see the

response of God to His wandering bride: "Behold, I will allure her, [I] will bring her into the wilderness, and speak comfort to her. I will give her her vineyards from there, and the Valley of Achor as a *door of hope;* she shall sing there, as in the days of her youth, as in the day when she came up from the land of Egypt" (Hos. 2:14–15). The Lord is opening this door to invite His people out of their captivity and compromise and into their true destiny. It's a door that leads us out of the Valley of Trouble and into renewed covenant with God. This door will lead the church from her compromise into betrothal and fruitfulness.

Finally, the last door being opened is the **Door of Heaven**. In the book of Revelation, John writes, "After these things I looked, and behold, a door standing open in heaven. And the first voice which I heard was like a trumpet speaking with me, saying, 'Come up here, and I will show you things which must take place after this'" (Rev. 4:1). The Lord, who invited John to come up higher for the heavenly perspective, is also inviting His church, His beloved, to "come up higher" and sit with Him around His throne. The invitation lifts us out of our compromised state and into the revelation of heaven's perspective. With heaven's perspective, we gain revelation regarding our identity and destiny in God. This door will help the church realize her transforming purpose.

These "doors" represent an invitation from Jesus to pass through them to new places of intimacy, freedom, and destiny. God is giving us keys that will unlock these doors, both in our personal lives and collectively for the sake of our cities. As we accept His invitation and pass through each door Jesus will lead us into our true identity as His bride and into our transforming purpose!

> *Lift up your heads, O you gates!*
> *And be lifted up, you everlasting doors!*
> *And the King of glory shall come in.*
> Psalm 24:7

# DOOR OF INTIMACY

"BEHOLD, I STAND AT THE DOOR
AND KNOCK. IF ANYONE HEARS MY
VOICE AND OPENS THE DOOR, I WILL
COME IN TO HIM AND DINE WITH
HIM, AND HE WITH ME."

REVELATION 3:20

## Chapter 1

# DESPERATE
# FOR HIS PRESENCE

"AS THE DEER PANTS FOR STREAMS OF WATER,
SO MY SOUL PANTS FOR YOU, O GOD. MY SOUL
THIRSTS FOR GOD, FOR THE LIVING GOD. WHEN
CAN I GO AND MEET WITH GOD?"

PSALM 42:1–2 NIV

"AMEN!" the pastor declares as the morning worship service concludes and the worship leader finishes playing the final song. It was a good service. There were a variety of interesting activities, including a drama presentation, an update on a missionary family serving overseas, the children's special song, and a report on the upcoming fund-raiser for the new youth center.

You watch people chat as they make their way to the door. Then you notice a woman who doesn't seem in a hurry to leave—isn't that the young mother who was recently divorced? Then you look a little more closely at the people leaving: the teenager with a blank, empty look on his face; the well-dressed man who is bravely facing a recent diagnosis of inoperable cancer; an elderly woman with kind but sad eyes. You wonder about deeper issues that are hidden—addictions, emotional bondages, fear of the future, loneliness, families torn by conflict. But these are the burdens you don't see when people carry them into the service and back out with them. Something tugs at your heart.

*What's wrong?* you think to yourself. *This was a normal service, nothing unusual; the worship was uplifting, the sermon encouraging.* There was the prayer time when you felt a moment of peace. You hope that somehow the peace will last a bit further into the week, at least past your Monday morning meeting. Reality begins to sink in, and your thoughts race ahead to the coming week.

You take one more look at the people leaving the sanctuary. Something is wrong, but you can't quite put your finger on it. You feel a longing in your heart for something more. You wonder if there is something missing, or maybe Someone . . .

## THE SILENT CRY FOR "ONE THING"

A widespread cry is growing in the hearts of believers for a real, tangible encounter with God. They want, like Moses, to see Him face-to-face. They don't want only to read about Him, talk about Him, and pay homage to Him on Sunday mornings. This strong undercurrent in our nation manifests itself as a holy dissatisfaction with the status quo of the institutional church. Many people who have attended church faithfully for years are now wandering around disconnected from any collective expression of the body of Christ. As mentioned in the Introduction, researcher George Barna estimates that more than ten million born-again believers in the United States are now considered "unchurched."[1] People have become disillusioned and jaded; many are unwilling to return to the local church in its current condition.

What are people longing for? I believe it's the presence of God in the midst of His people, the manifestation of His nearness, and an awareness of His love that is both real and relevant. We desperately need the tangible presence of Jesus both in the church and in our communities!

How do we gauge whether or not His presence is among us? Do we simply *assume* He is present? This is a fair question. *How do we know?* Should we even ask the question? I'm not referring to the omnipresence of God but to His *manifest* presence. Do we believe Jesus is present simply because we wish Him to be there? Or is there discernible evidence when He is present and when He is absent?

God is looking for people with a heart like David, who declared, "*One thing* I have desired of the Lord, that will I seek: that I may dwell in the house of the Lord all the days of my life, to behold the beauty of the Lord, and to inquire in His temple" (Ps. 27:4, emphasis added).

People who are desperate for God's presence move beyond convenience and personal comfort. They have gotten hold of something in their spirit, and they cannot let go. For them, Jesus is not a religious concept—He is reality. The very fact that Jesus came to live among us is a clear example of His desire to be with us in a way that we can both understand and pursue.

## DESPERATE HUNGER

An initial hunger and thirst comes with the gift of salvation, but after the spiritual honeymoon is over, we must intentionally cultivate our spiritual passion. Recognizing that we may have grown cold in our love toward Him, our first prayer must be to ask

> DESPERATE HUNGER IS THE CURRENCY OF HEAVEN.

Him to increase our spiritual appetite. Jesus warns us that in the last days the love of many would grow cold (Matthew 24:12). We must commit to our pursuit of His presence and accept His invitation for real relationship and intimacy.

Jesus makes this invitation clear in Revelation, chapter 3. Writing to the church of Laodicea, He challenges their lukewarmness by saying, "You say 'I am rich; I have become wealthy, and have need of nothing'—and do not know that you are wretched, miserable, poor, blind, and naked" (Rev. 3:17).

His counsel to the compromised church is: "Buy from Me gold refined in the fire, that you may be rich; white garments that you may be clothed, that the shame of your nakedness may not be revealed; and anoint your eyes with eye salve, that you may see" (Rev. 3:18).

How do we buy this gold from Jesus? What type of currency allows us to buy pure gold in exchange for our "wretched" condition? The answer is hunger. Desperate hunger is the currency of heaven. Hunger is what causes us to empty ourselves of compromise and creates a holy dissatisfaction that drives us to our knees and makes us depend on God.

We cannot be hungry for God if we are being satisfied with other things. Because the church constantly "nibbles" on "junk food" from the world, she has lost her appetite for God. We don't even feel the pain of hunger for Him; we are starving for lack of His presence without even knowing it. In order to make room for Him in our lives, we must empty our hearts and set aside our own agendas. Before we can be filled, we must be emptied!

The best way to be emptied is to cultivate a life of spiritual hunger and remove all traces of self-satisfaction. The greater the capacity on the inside, the more desperate our hunger will be for God. We have settled for so much less than He wants to give us of himself!

Our relationship with Him cannot simply be added to our life like an appendage. He is not a lucky charm we carry in our pocket to protect us from bad things or bring us good fortune. He is God! He doesn't fit into our little boxes and our self-centered agendas. God wants to fill us to overflowing with who He is—to conform us to the image of His Son—and then pour us out into the lives of the people in our communities. In all too many churches today we are confronted with the reality of Isaiah 64:7: "There is no one who calls on Your name, who stirs himself up to take hold of You."

The lack of desperate longing for God has brought us to our present condition. The stale quality of our religious lives is a direct result of our lack of holy desire. Jesus waits to be seriously wanted and invited. In response, we must trade our complacency for abandonment. He promises that those who hunger and thirst after righteousness shall be filled (Matt. 5:6). Let us ask the Lord to "salt our hearts" and cause a fresh hunger and thirst to overtake us. He will give us as much of himself as we ask for!

## RUNNING TO THE ALTARS

I witnessed a powerful example of desperate spiritual hunger during an international revival conference in Argentina. That evening, as evangelist Carlos Annacondia preached to eight thousand people in a stadium, the air was filled with anticipation. God had already done many marvelous things during the conference. Leaders who had traveled from more than forty nations waited to be touched by the power and goodness of God.

The floor of the stadium could hold only five thousand people standing, so we knew it would be interesting to see what would happen when Annacondia invited them forward to pray. Sure enough, as the evangelist closed his message, and before he actually gave the invitation, people quietly began to move toward the stadium floor and creep along the wall toward the platform. It was fun to watch. Soon the "creepers" grew in number. Undaunted by the polite request to keep the stadium floor clear, they had done the calculations and knew that all eight thousand people couldn't fit on the floor. As a result, they made a decision. Because of their desperate hunger for God, they decided that no matter what it took, they would get to that altar and receive prayer!

Then it happened: When Carlos Annacondia issued the invitation to come to the altar, the crowd surged forward. Within seconds five thousand hungry people pressed in tightly on the stadium floor, hands raised, crying out to God. I heard a testimony from a pastor later who said when the power of God fell on the crowd, it felt like a lightning bolt had struck his head. He remembered thinking, *"This is going to kill me!"*

At the same time another interesting situation was unfolding up in the bleachers. I had to walk up and out of the stadium during the altar call, and as I did so a small group of leaders from the United States grabbed my arm and stopped me. "We have traveled thousands of miles and spent a lot of money to come to this conference to have Carlos Annacondia pray for us," they shouted. "Now look! The floor is already filled, and there is no way we can get to him!"

They were important leaders, and I knew I should be helpful as their host. But as I looked down at the floor packed with hungry people getting touched by God, the only thing I could think of was *Well, you need to learn to run to the altar!* As many others had literally run forward in their desperate hunger for God, these guys were all still sitting comfortably in their chairs. We had no way of keeping the "creepers" from getting there first, nor were we interested in policing spiritually hungry people to make room for those who felt "entitled" to be there.

The realization struck me that some people expect special treatment. They want the presence of God brought to them. They want it to be easy. I started noticing this same attitude in other cities where I traveled and ministered. We in the Western world aren't so willing to run to the altar. We expect God's glory to come to us on our terms and in our timing. God is not our butler, but sometimes we treat Him like one! When He hasn't served up revival in our way and on our schedule, we conclude that it is not going to come. Subsequently, we go about our business and then compensate for the lack of God's manifest presence with distracting activities or entertaining events.

## WHAT ARE WE HUNGRY FOR?

The issue is a lack of hunger—desperate, aching, unspeakable hunger for His presence! How hungry are we? We say we are hungry for God, but are we? What are we hungry for? What are we filling ourselves with? If we are already full of the lesser pleasures of this world, how can we have an appetite for God?

We must abandon ourselves to the pursuit of God until the nature of Jesus is formed within us and His life flows out of us like a river. We must become desperate in our search for God!

The pursuit of God's presence is costly! It requires sacrifice, diligence, and time. And this means that we must make choices about how we live our lives. Perhaps the amount of God's presence we experience is directly related to the sacrifice we pour out. Jesus wants to be "found" by us! God is trying to get our attention, to reveal himself to us, to communicate with us. As we intentionally pursue His presence in our lives, our hearts become tenderized by His love and our capacity to know Him increases. Intimate fellowship with God makes our hearts receptive to further revelation of His nature. We have within us the ability to know Him if we will but respond to His invitation.

Jesus promises in John 7:37–38, "If anyone thirsts, let him come to Me and drink. He who believes in Me, as the Scripture has said, out of his heart will flow rivers of living water." *Anyone!* If you are thirsty, you qualify! It is the rightful inheritance of every believer to have a heart overflowing with the Living Water of the Holy Spirit. This is a promise Jesus sets forth in His Word.

Our thirst for God can be quenched by lesser things, and we must be intentional to guard that thirst according to the warning in Proverbs 4:23: "Keep your heart with all diligence, for out of it spring the issues of life." The Scripture makes it clear that this river flows out of the believer; that means that what God pours into you is intended to flow out from you. There is a big difference between a river and a lake! God intends that there be an ongoing reality in our lives of thirst for God—being poured out and then becoming thirsty again.

People who are desperately hungry will do almost anything to satisfy that hunger. Those who are willing to move out of their normal routine and circumstances to seek the presence of God will not be disappointed.

## THE ROLE OF REVIVAL

Throughout Scripture and church history, we see numerous examples of God graciously sending revival to His people to restore spiritual hunger, life, and righteousness. Oftentimes revival comes at a very low point, when it's hard to find the discernable presence of the Lord among His people.

In the Old Testament, we can see a repeated cycle of God interacting with His people in supernatural ways that established them as His covenant people. In the book of Judges, for example, seasons of revival and supernatural interventions of God were followed by periods of spiritual decline that eventually led to apostasy and judgment, captivity and death. Successive generations would repent and cry out to God for deliverance; God would hear their cry and answer by raising up an anointed deliverer. Then Israel would experience a time of revival and restoration. But when the people would again drift away from God, break covenant, and turn to idolatry, spiritual decline and judgment would follow. In the midst of this recurring pattern in the Old Testament, there was always a remnant of people who remained faithful to God. They carried faith and hope in their hearts during dark times. Through their faithful lives God would ignite another revival when He wanted to restore spiritual life to His people.

In the New Testament, revival is not a prominent theme because the New Testament church *was still experiencing* revived Christianity. The church in the book of Acts is an example of a people in covenant with God, filled with faith and power, and having a tremendous impact on their society.

Within a couple of generations, however, the Old Testament pattern evident in the book of Judges reappears in Christianity, and the cycle of spiritual decline among God's people becomes a prominent feature of church history. The Western world hasn't experienced a sweeping revival for almost one hundred years. As we will see evidenced in later chapters, when the church continues on in her programs without the tangible presence of Jesus, her ministry is not effective and the world around her is not impressed but bored.

When God withdraws His presence, it serves to stimulate spiritual hunger again, something we are beginning to see in the Western world. Since our generation has never witnessed a nation-wide spiritual awakening, we have little understanding of the magnitude of the impact of God's presence among us, which hinders our motivation to pray earnestly for it.

In the book *The Fire of God's Presence* Wesley Adams describes what God's glory looks like when poured out on entire communities:

> This is revival from Heaven!—When men in the streets are afraid to speak godless words for fear that God's judgment will fall! When sinners, aware of the fire of God's presence, tremble in the streets and cry out for mercy! When, without human advertising, the Holy Spirit sweeps across cities and towns in supernatural power and holds people in the grip of terrifying conviction. When every store becomes a pulpit, every heart an altar, every home a sanctuary, and people walk carefully before God—this is revival![2]

## DIVINE MAGNETISM

When God manifests His presence in a city or region, people are drawn by the divine magnetism of His presence. Throughout history God's manifest presence has caused great numbers of people to come together to hear the gospel. When John the Baptist preached in the wilderness, people from Jerusalem and the surrounding area flocked to hear his prophetic message, repent of their sins, and be baptized. What drew the people? It is difficult to explain such drawing power apart from the magnetism of the Holy Spirit.

Dr. Wesley Adams writes,

> Wherever genuine revival occurs, people are drawn there, not by clever advertising or human persuasion, but by the magnetism of God's manifest presence. It was so in 18th century England when 20,000 people gathered in Newcastle upon the Tyne to hear John Wesley (an out of town stranger) preach in the open air on Isaiah 53.

This same magnetism drew thousands of coal miners to the fields of Kingswood near Bristol, England in 1739 to hear George White-field and John Wesley preach the word with authority and anointing during the beginnings of revival.

This same kind of supernatural magnetism drew thousands to previously empty churches in New York City in 1857, in Wales in 1904 and in the Hebrides in 1949. People in great numbers bowed in humility, repentance of sin and a righteous fear of God as they encountered God's mercy and forgiveness and experienced the joy of salvation. Church buildings with their multiple services each night could not accommodate all the people who came. People could no longer be indifferent to God and what He was doing. People could still resist God and respond negatively to His invitation of mercy, as some people did, but they could no longer view God as unimportant, irrelevant or coldly detached from current history. The reality of God and His salvation was like a blazing fire with amazing drawing power.[3]

## TRANSFORMATION—THE OUTWORKING OF REVIVAL

The presence of God in the midst of people has always been the catalyst for change. Jesus is the Redeemer and Restorer of all things. No meaningful or lasting change can occur without His involvement. On the contrary, without His presence among us we are left to stale experience and empty, ineffective institutions.

Because revival is intended to be a catalyst for the church, revivals are not sustainable in and of themselves. Revivals release "new wine" to the church, but Jesus said that if you put new wine in old wine-skins, they cannot contain it and they will burst. The container or "wineskin" must also be changed to prepare to contain what God desires to pour out, both in our individual lives and in our communities.

Until recently we spoke of God coming to a community only in terms of "revival." We have hoped that somehow God would "choose us" and decide to send a powerful revival to our church or community. Sometimes God does send a brief revival, but such revivals are short-lived and unfortunately don't have much impact on society as a whole. Recent revivals have brought much-needed refreshing and healing to the church, but the discouraging reality of revival in history is that it doesn't last for very long unless it results in spiritual

awakening in the community. While it serves as a catalyst to return
the church to righteousness and purpose, its impact is not necessarily
felt in the community.

In 1999 George Otis Jr., founder and president of The Sentinel
Group, released a video entitled *Transformations*.[4] It was a documen-
tary of several supernaturally transformed communities—places
where the presence of God had descended into a community and
brought real, long-lasting change. People were stunned by what they
saw on the video, and a new hope and faith began to stir in the hearts
of God's people. This documentation of transformation has become
a hot topic in the church today: What is transformation exactly? How
do you get it? Why does God choose some places to demonstrate His
presence and glory so dramatically and not others? It has caused many
of us to long for more and to press into the Lord with a new fervency
in intercession for God's presence to touch our community. Having
believed the amazing report of God's activity around the world,
people in many communities are now asking the questions, "Why
not here?" "Why not now?" "Why not us?"

George continued his pursuit of God's transformation activities
and has since released several more videos highlighting the unprecedented frequency of activity of the Holy Spirit in communities
around the world. What he has discovered is powerful evidence that
God wants to do more than revive us—He wants to transform us *and*
the communities we live in.

What is city transformation? *City transformation results from desperate people unifying in vision and intercession, enabling the heavens to "open"
over a city.* The result is revival in the church and spiritual awakening
in the city. According to Otis, transformation is

> a neighborhood or city whose values and institutions are overrun
> by God. Divine fire has not only been summoned, it has fallen. It
> is a culture that has been impacted by the full measure of the King-
> dom of God. A society in which supernatural power flows like a
> river of molten lava, altering everything and everyone in its path.[5]

Each community God touches is unique in its journey toward
transformation. You cannot predict which way things will go or
when the breakthrough will come, but there are common principles

from God's Word that serve as important foundations for the transformation journey. Rather than trying to draw up a "plan" from where God has worked before, we must discover these same biblical principles in our own lives and communities and trust God to lead us.

The critical component to revival in the church and transformation in the community is the manifest presence of Jesus. In transformed communities, the presence of God is a valued and critical component of the well-being of the community at every level of society. Participants in transformation in these communities include presidents, prime ministers, mayors, businessmen, law enforcement officers, clergy, and laypeople. People from all over the world are gathering to cry out to God and labor together to seek His presence and the transformation of their communities.

We must become hungry and thirsty for more of Jesus in our midst. We must cry out in desperation for God's presence to be restored in our lives, our churches, and ultimately in our cities. We must treasure the manifest presence of God, because as Jesus said in John 15:5, "Without Me you can do nothing."

# Chapter 2

# THE GLORY
# OF HIS PRESENCE

"AND THE WORD BECAME FLESH AND DWELT
AMONG US, AND WE BEHELD HIS GLORY, THE
GLORY AS OF THE ONLY BEGOTTEN OF THE
FATHER, FULL OF GRACE AND TRUTH."

JOHN 1:14

The universal presence of God is a fact. God is here! The whole universe is alive with His life! He is no strange or foreign god but the familiar Father of our Lord Jesus Christ, whose love has pursued humanity throughout history.

The Bible refers to the glory of God in several ways. Sometimes it describes God's splendor and majesty (1 Chronicles 29:11; Habakkuk 3:3–5). God's glory in this sense is so great that no human being can see it and live (see Exodus 33:18–33). The glory of God is directly related to His uniqueness, His holiness (Isaiah 6:1–3), and His transcendence (Romans 11:36; Hebrews 13:21).

Another aspect of God's glory in the Bible is His supernatural presence and power being revealed. The glory of the Lord is referred to nineteen times in the book of Ezekiel. The book begins with a prophetic description of the glory of God:

Above the expanse over their heads was what looked like a throne of sapphire, and high above on the throne was a figure like that of a man. I saw that from what appeared to be his waist up he looked like glowing metal, as if full of fire, and that from there down he looked like fire; and brilliant light surrounded him. Like the appearance of a rainbow in the clouds on a rainy day, so was the radiance around him. This was the appearance of the *likeness of the glory of the Lord.* (Ezekiel 1:26–28 NIV, emphasis added)

*Only His likeness*—imagine what the fullness of His glory would be like!

A third way the Bible depicts the glory of God is through His visible presence among His people, called the *Shekinah* glory. The Hebrew word *Shekinah* refers to the dwelling of God and describes the visible manifestation of His presence and glory (Ex. 13:21).

The New Testament equivalent of the Old Testament *Shekinah* glory is Jesus Christ. John tells us, "And the Word became flesh and dwelt among us, and we beheld His glory, the glory as of the only begotten of the Father, full of grace and truth" (John 1:14). When people saw Jesus, they saw the glory of God!

"Now the dwelling of God is with men, and he will live with them. They will be his people, and God himself will be with them and be their God" (Rev. 21:3 NIV).

## MANIFEST PRESENCE

God's presence manifests itself in different ways. Psalm 19 speaks of how He reveals His glory through creation: "The heavens declare the glory of God; and the firmament shows His handiwork." Then, individually, the Holy Spirit indwells every believer, and we become the temple of His presence. The Bible says that when believers gather together, the Lord will be "in the midst of them" (Matt. 18:20).

What about His tangible presence in our midst today? Where is His glory?

In his book *God's Favorite House* Tommy Tenney points out that much of what we experience today in our public worship gatherings is general grace and blessing. Granted, we should be thankful for that. But it's not the fullness of what God intends for us when we gather together. A startling difference exists between God's general grace and His manifest presence and glory. The grace of God that rests on our ministry is about us; the glory is about Him. God gives grace and blessing to make our preaching, singing, and praying more effective spiritually. When He blesses our ministry, it empowers human gifts, talents, and callings with the power of God. *Nevertheless, it is still resting on the flesh.* We have settled for a token of God's presence when He wants us to experience the fullness of His presence through the Holy Spirit.[1]

> OUR PROGRAMS, EVENTS, AND ACTIVITIES HAVE BECOME SUBSTITUTES FOR HIS PRESENCE.

When the manifest presence of Jesus is absent, we turn instead to programs, methods, organizations, and an assortment of activities to occupy our time and attention. Our programs, events, and activities have become substitutes for His presence. No wonder the Christian experience is judged as being empty and not very interesting. These things can never satisfy the longing of a human heart. "The shallowness of our inner experience, the hollowness of our worship, and the servile imitation of the world that marks our promotional methods all testify that we, in this day, know God only imperfectly, and the peace of God scarcely at all."[2]

## PRESENCE-DRIVEN?

Today it is rare to find a church where the manifest presence of Jesus is the primary attraction or sustaining focus. Instead, we are utilizing many methods for "successful" church growth. But in spite of our best efforts and the time, energy, and resources invested, the life-changing encounter with our beautiful, powerful God is missing.

It would appear that the corporate church today has made an erroneous conclusion—that her ministry is no longer absolutely dependent upon the evidential reality of Christ's presence. A theology of His abiding presence has replaced hunger for and the pursuit of His glorious manifest presence. In our presumption, we have left our dependence upon an intimate partnership with Jesus, and the church is blazing her own trail. But where is this trail leading us?

The journal *Ministries Today* devoted an article to the subject of pursuing God's presence:

> God's presence precedes and permeates all other models of church growth. Without His presence, church growth is simply a

menagerie of methodologies doomed to temporality. A method may work for the moment, but shouldn't our desire be to do only that which has eternal impact?

The article goes on to say:

> Going back to our roots in Scripture, being presence-driven literally derives from Ephesians 5:18, where Paul instructs us to "be filled with the Spirit." The filling referred to here projects the image of a sail being filled with the wind (the *ruwach,* or wind of God). The breath of God's Spirit must fill the church, empowering it to move forward into God's destiny.
>
> God's Spirit births every movement of the church. Without being Spirit- or presence-driven, the church sits listlessly in time, like a sailboat going nowhere in a calm sea. We can use our paradigm as paddles and row as hard as we like, but the forward progress is negligible. Or, we can hoist our sails of worship, catch the wind of His Spirit and move forward into His purpose, plans and productivity (fruit) in ministry.[3]

A modern-day example of God's presence ministering to a vast array of people is the Azusa Street Revival in 1906. Arguably, this humble revival had the most pervasive influence around the world of any revival in history up to that time. The revival was marked by powerful encounters with God's presence. Unsuspecting, hungry individuals were swept up in God's presence. The following excerpt provides a glimpse of their experience with God:

> The services ran almost continuously. Seeking souls could be found under the power almost any hour, night and day. The place was never closed nor empty. The people came to meet God. He was always there. Hence the continuous meeting. The meeting did not depend on the human leader. God's presence became more and more wonderful. In that old building, with its low rafters and bare floors, God took strong men and women to pieces, and put them together again, for His glory. It was a tremendous overhauling process. Pride and self-assertion, self-importance and self-esteem, could not survive there. The religious ego preached its own funeral quickly.

We saw some wonderful things in those days. Even very good men came to abhor themselves in the clearer light of God. The preachers died the hardest. They had so much to die to. So much reputation and good works. But when God got through with them they gladly turned a new page and chapter. That was one reason they fought so hard. Death is not at all a pleasant experience. And strong men die hard.

The meetings started themselves, spontaneously, in testimony, praise and worship. We had no prearranged program to be jammed through on time. Our time was the Lord's. We had real testimonies, from fresh heart-experiences. Otherwise, the shorter the testimonies, the better. A dozen might be on their feet at once, trembling under the mighty power of God. We did not have to get our cue from leaders. And we were free from lawlessness. We were shut up to God in prayer in the meetings, our minds on Him.[4]

In every revival in history we read a similar testimony. When God responded to His people by sending His presence, He didn't just work himself into their routine religion—He overtook them by His power and glory! He left a trail of glorious chaos in His wake—weeping, repenting, rejoicing, reconciling, changing of habits, healing families! Nobody wondered if Jesus was involved in these meetings. There was no doubt in their minds and no lack in their hearts.

## WHOSE PRESENCE ARE WE TRYING TO ATTRACT?

GOD'S PRESENCE IS MORE EFFECTIVE THAN OUR BEST CHURCH GROWTH METHODS.

We have many methods and plans about how to make people feel welcome in the church. Many of those methods are successful in drawing people, but are they drawing the presence of the Lord? The presence of Jesus always has been and always will be what is most attractive for hungry people. For long-term success, we must build something that attracts His presence.

When God's presence becomes a tangible reality in a community, the church then becomes a catalyst for growth. God's presence is more effective than our best church growth methods. When God's presence is tangible, supernatural ministry results and becomes a magnet for hungry souls and broken people. In his book *Revival Fire*

Wesley Duewel makes the noteworthy statement, "God's presence and power are so mightily and extensively at work during revival that God accomplishes more in hours or days than usually results from years of faithful ministry without His presence."[5]

Shouldn't Jesus himself be the preeminent attraction? We can promote our church programs with precision and good marketing techniques, but when somebody who is blind or deaf gets healed, or a political leader gets saved, or once-barren land produces a bountiful harvest, people will flock to the church. God is His own best promoter! He just shows up and effortlessly turns our routines into supernatural encounters that are life changing.

## PURSUIT OF HIS PRESENCE

The pursuit of God's presence is not a means to an end. *It is the end!* What we are talking about is not a formula for how to be more effective in ministry. It is the core of our existence and the purpose of our life. We exist to know Him, to worship Him, and to reflect His beauty to the world around us!

God is waiting and longing for us to experience an awareness of His presence. Knowing His presence in theory but not in experience is not biblical faith. It is religion only. We have the privilege as believers to know and experience the tangible presence of God!

In *The Pursuit of God,* A. W. Tozer makes a contrast between being in the presence of God *positionally* and experiencing His presence *actually.* He goes on to say that, as a result of settling for the positional presence of God only, contentment takes the place of burning hearts and fervent zeal for the Lord. "The church then settles for only an intellectual knowledge of God and remains unconcerned about the absence of personal experience."[6]

## GOD INITIATES THE PURSUIT

If our pursuit of God is successful, it's only because He has initiated the pursuit. God wants to make himself known to us and meet with us. An important doctrine of Christian theology is that of "prevenient grace," which means that before a person can seek God, God must first cause the hunger and initiate the grace to make possible the seeking. And before a sinful man can have a right understanding about God, the Lord must grant some measure of understanding to his heart.

We can pursue God only because He has created a longing in our hearts to know Him. It takes God to cause us to pursue God! "No one can come to Me unless the Father who sent Me draws him" (John 6:44). Our good intentions simply aren't enough; we cannot stir up anything in and of ourselves. We are desperately dependent upon God even for our faith to pursue Him! The desire to pursue God may begin with God, but the degree to which we find Him is up to us. The good news is that God has created people with not only the capacity but also the instinct to seek after Him.

Why do some people seem to experience God's presence in deeper ways than others? We all know people who are full of spiritual life and seem to be closely connected to God. We also know others who never seem to be able to connect to Him on a deep level. Why is that? God's desire is to relate to each of us in intimate fellowship. He offers all of us the same invitation to fellowship with Him. The problem, therefore, is not with God but with how people relate to God; it's not a matter of distance but experience.

The important distinction that is present in people who have experienced God is spiritual hunger. People who are hungry for more of God "press in" to Him. Like the woman who pressed through the crowds to take hold of Jesus' garment and was healed, and like the blind man who cried out to Jesus in spite of the disciples' rebuke to keep quiet—such people are not content until they have actually been touched by Him.

It's not enough to *feel* spiritual hunger, we must *do* something about it! People who encounter Jesus in a tangible way have not only made room for God in their lives, He has become their life! They, like the woman who poured the perfume on the feet of Jesus, are willing to give everything to Him as an act of worship.

## OUR STORY

God spoke through the prophet Isaiah that He would come to earth and call himself *Immanuel*—"God with us." God longs to be with us! God named himself after the intention of His heart! The Father sent His only Son, Jesus, who chose to die rather than to live apart from us. How could God make His intention any clearer? What an amazing day it is when we come face-to-face with the God who loves us! He becomes *our* Immanuel!

In the history of God's people, we find seasons of right fellowship with God and seasons of idolatry, years of captivity and times of restoration. It began in the Garden of Eden with Adam and Eve. Until sin entered the Garden, they enjoyed perfect fellowship with God and each other. As a result of sin, they lost this intimate fellowship with God. In their shame, they tried to hide from God.

Humanity's story concludes in the book of Revelation in the city of the New Jerusalem, where God again dwells in intimate fellowship with His redeemed family. This is not just an ancient story—it's our story as well. When our love for God grows cold and our faith wanes, we wander away from Him too. We are living between the Garden of Eden and the New Jerusalem.

The ongoing story of humanity is of people wandering away, but being pursued by a loving God who created us for fellowship with Him. Who can flee from His presence when He fills the entire universe?

God's desire for relationship has never changed. The Creator of the universe, the One who has always existed, longs to be with us! He longs for relationship and fellowship with us as people. The Lord promises in Jeremiah: "You will seek Me and find Me, when you search for Me with all your heart. I will be found by you, says the Lord" (Jer. 29:13–14). God has never stopped pursuing His people.

All of creation waits for the day of final redemption (Rom. 8:19). That day awaits our task of filling cities with the testimony of Jesus and seeing them transformed from within by divine grace. The whole Bible is a picture of regaining what was lost—restoration and redemption not only of individuals but of entire communities.

## Surprise Encounter

In 1990 I was living what I thought was a full and satisfying Christian life—I had good friends, a great job, and meaningful ministry in my church. Then one night at a service I sensed a clear invitation from the Lord to serve Him for a year as a short-term missionary in another country. One year later I found myself on a mission assignment in Buenos Aires, Argentina. I thought the adventure of faith I had embarked on was about the external experience of living the life of a missionary. I quickly realized, however, that the journey I had agreed to was about something far deeper—my understanding of who God is and what a life of faith is really about: An adventure with a very real, very faithful, and very unpredictable God!

While working at a national Bible institute that trained students for ministry, I found an almost constant tangible presence of the Lord on the campus. My encounter with the Lord in Argentina surprised me. This was something I neither looked for nor expected. But God's presence was unmistakably there, and it changed my life.

Every day during chapel service the presence of God could be felt. I remember feeling waves of His presence moving over the hundreds of students as they poured out their hearts in worship and sacrifice before Him. Spending time with Jesus was the highest priority of that Bible institute. Jesus knew He was welcome there, and He took full advantage of it!

God wasn't a surprise guest. He wasn't an unexpected visitor. He was the reason we went to chapel—to worship and encounter Him. We didn't do anything special or unusual to get Him to come. We didn't work up some emotional climate; there was no hype. He just liked to dwell among us. Why did the Lord apparently enjoy "hanging out" on the campus? I believe it was because the students made a place for Him in their hearts and lives. They prepared a dwelling place for His presence, and He came in such a way that everyone was aware of it.

An interesting consequence of the manifest presence of the Lord was His ministry among us. We were content just to worship Him, but sometimes people were healed, emotionally and physically, during our worship services. The students were desperate for God; many had given everything they had to study at the school, and many of us depended completely on the Lord for our provision. We led very simple lives, but we had Jesus, and His presence sustained us, encouraged us, healed us, and empowered us for ministry. There was no lack, no other passion, just utter dependence on God and the resulting joy of making Him the center of our lives.

When I returned to the United States, I had a difficult time adjusting back to our church culture and I was depressed for six months. It wasn't just leaving my friends in Argentina and a city that I had come to love. I missed the presence of Jesus that I had there! I couldn't "find" Him in the familiar places where He was "supposed" to be, places where I had been content in my relationship with Him before. It wasn't the same anymore. I was hungry now. I wanted more of Him and the manifest reality of His presence. I felt like the breath had been knocked out of me.

The strange thing was that nobody else seemed to notice His absence. As I entered back into my familiar routine, I realized how much I had been missing but never knew it. It was just how things were. I remember sitting in church one Sunday morning and the service ended, just when it was supposed to end. I watched people stream out of the sanctuary, my heart pounding. I wanted to shout to all of them, "Wait! You can't leave! Jesus hasn't shown up yet!" I looked around and saw people in need of healing or deliverance; nobody had been saved that morning. Why were we stopping the service? Why did we even *have* the service if it wasn't to encounter Jesus?

My experience in Argentina was a wake-up call for my Christian life. It caused me to begin asking questions, mostly about my own spiritual life, but also about the church in general. Those questions led me on a new journey with the Lord in pursuit of His presence and resulted in a fresh spiritual hunger that has grown through the years. Something happens in us when we taste His presence; nothing else satisfies anymore. Everything that used to matter so much now pales in comparison.

## REFLECTORS OF HIS GLORY

When Moses returned from his awesome encounter with the Lord on Mount Sinai, his face reflected the glory of the Lord. It was so intense that he had to put a veil over his face to protect the Israelites, but it eventually faded away. Paul, in 2 Corinthians 3:7–9, says that under the new covenant we should expect an even *greater* degree of glory than was witnessed on the face of Moses!

We need a fresh glimpse of Jesus, to "behold His glory" (John 1:14). We are transformed by that beholding. We are changed into the likeness of what we behold. Paul talks about the transformation that results from our fixed gaze upon Jesus in these words: "We, who with unveiled faces all reflect the Lord's glory, are being transformed into his likeness with ever-increasing glory" (2 Cor. 3:18 NIV). God is most glorified when we are living abundant lives and reflecting His glory (John 10:10).

We can only reflect what we have been beholding. If we aren't encountering the real, tangible presence of the Lord and "beholding His glory," how can we become a reflector of His glory in our communities?

Have you ever experienced the presence of God in a tangible way? Have you felt His presence draw near during a worship service or a personal prayer time? We will give ourselves fully to those things we are passionate about. The question is, what are we desiring? What has gained our attention and captured our hearts?

## Chapter 3

# THE LOVE OF OUR KING

"I PRAY THAT YOU, BEING ROOTED AND
ESTABLISHED IN LOVE, MAY HAVE POWER,
TOGETHER WITH ALL THE SAINTS, TO GRASP
HOW WIDE AND LONG AND HIGH AND DEEP IS
THE LOVE OF CHRIST, AND TO KNOW THIS LOVE
THAT SURPASSES KNOWLEDGE—THAT YOU MAY
BE FILLED TO THE MEASURE OF ALL THE
FULLNESS OF GOD."

EPHESIANS 3:17–19 NIV

The purpose of desperation and spiritual hunger is to draw us into a more intimate relationship with Jesus both personally and corporately. That deepened relationship in turn releases a greater revelation of God's love. Loving and being loved by God is the greatest joy a person can experience—it's what we were created for!

Another joy of knowing Jesus is that we as His body can become carriers of His love and presence into our families, workplaces, and communities. We can only bring out into the community what God has first worked in us. Jesus must become a reality in His body before His body can take that reality to the city. What a privilege to be an ambassador for the King! We are called to be "ministers of reconciliation" (2 Cor. 5:18) and to represent His kingdom with all its love, compassion, power, and healing.

Throughout the Bible, church history, and even today in the evidential transformation of hundreds of communities across the world, we see that God's presence is required to effect a real and tangible change in society. As the people of God we have a responsibility to cry out for His presence to fill our communities. God is longing to be invited into our communities so that He can bring love, life, healing, and restoration to a people without hope.

To exist without the revelation of the love of God is to be barren and desolate. That barrenness and desolation then manifests itself in tangible ways in our communities. Our communities are typically full of broken families, immorality, corruption, and violence, reflecting a place where there is darkness and every evil practice. Every day people are betrayed, rejected, ignored, violated, and abused somewhere in our cities.

Why should we be surprised at our city's condition? How can there be any life without love? *Love is a Person!* Without the tangible presence of Jesus dwelling among His people, there can be no joy, mercy, compassion, power, healing, or restoration. In John 15:13, it says there is no greater love than that a man lay down his life for his friends. As believers in the Lord Jesus Christ, it is our responsibility to love.

Do you ever wonder why people aren't lining up to come to our church services? Could it be we aren't offering people life that flows out of love? Could it be we are offering them a substitute they find unappealing and unsatisfying? I don't believe the reputation of the church in most communities is one of love. Many non-Christians feel judged by the church or marketed to by the church, but not loved.

Laborers in our churches are growing weak in love with subsequent burnout and compromise. Why? Because we have disconnected from our Source of life and love. Ministry has ceased to be an overflow of our intimate relationship with Jesus; consequently it bears the slick sheen of professionalism. We are more concerned about the plans of men than the plans of God, and more concerned about attracting people than attracting God.

## THE LOVE OF GOD

The teachers of the law asked Jesus, "Of all the commandments, which is the most important?" Jesus answered that love for God was the first and most important of all the commandments. He added that the second most important commandment was to "love your neighbor as yourself." Then Jesus concluded: "There is no commandment greater than these" (Mark 12:28–31 NIV).

True love is both vertical (God's love for us and our love for God) and horizontal (God's love in us released to others). Our purpose is not only to be saved from our sins and their eternal consequences. Our purpose is also about pursuing God with an abandoned heart and discovering His limitless beauty and glory. Redemption is not only about God taking care of the negative equation of sin; it is also about His ultimate plan for His creation that involves the King's love for His people and their reciprocal love for Him.

Who is this King of Glory? What kind of a king would offer His love to receive the weak, immature love of a human being? John 3:16 says that God loved us so much that He sent His only Son to die on the cross to restore fellowship with us. He didn't just want our allegiance (which He could have demanded)—He wants our love.

We're not slaves any longer or even just friends. The revelation of the church at the end of the age is that of a bride. That level of intimacy is much deeper and only that level of intimacy is going to sustain us in the days ahead. It's our confidence in God's love that will allow us to stand firm and not be shaken.

God is preparing His family, His body to become the perfect, spotless bride for His Son. The whole gospel is about a romance! The story begins in the Garden with a marriage between Adam and Eve and ends in the book of Revelation with a marriage between Jesus and His bride—the church. The motivation behind everything God does is love. The love of God is so vast that it is incomprehensible in its scope and depth. It comes with one prerequisite, however: the love must be exclusive. It is not offered to us as one of many choices.

A. W. Tozer said, "God formed us for His pleasure, and so formed us that we, as well as He, can, in divine communion, enjoy the sweet and mysterious mingling of kindred personalities. He meant for us to see Him and live with Him and draw our life from His smile."[1]

The Song of Solomon is filled with highly emotional language. This beautiful book depicts the love story of a man and woman, but it also paints a word picture of our relationship with Christ, our Bridegroom. The Lord desires us! He is knocking at our door. He is pursuing us. Jesus is stirring the heart of His bride today to return to Him with mutual love, longing, and desire. Psalm 45:11 says, "So the King will greatly desire your beauty; because He is your Lord, worship Him."

In our intellectual church culture, we don't talk much about God's emotions. We shy away from being emotional about God ourselves because we are afraid of emotionalism or hype. But our relationship with God is meant to be intimate in a spiritual sense. In the fifth chapter of Ephesians Paul likens the church's intimacy with Christ to that of a human marriage. What would a marriage be like without intimacy, emotion, and real love? It would be cold, stoic, impersonal, and mechanical. This is not a picture of a healthy marriage, nor is it a healthy picture of the church in its relationship to Christ!

## A KNOCK AT THE DOOR

The Lord is the initiator of love. He is always the first to extend the invitation for fellowship and intimacy. We are the ones who hesitate. Look at the interaction between the beloved, representing the Lord, and the bride in the Song of Solomon:

> I sleep, but my heart is awake; it is the voice of my beloved! He knocks, saying, "Open for me, my sister, my love, my dove, my perfect one; for my head is covered with dew, my locks with the drops of the night" (Song of Solomon 5:2).

The bride is stirred by the voice of her bridegroom and his knock at the door, but she hesitates.

> I have taken off my robe; how can I put it on again? I have washed my feet; how can I defile them? (v. 3)

The bride has become too comfortable. Although her heart leaped at the sound of his voice, getting up to open the door for him seems inconvenient. By the time she changes her mind, he is already gone.

> I opened for my beloved, but my beloved had turned away and was gone. My heart leaped up when he spoke. I sought him, but I could not find him; I called him, but he gave me no answer. (v. 6)

Isn't this an accurate depiction of how we often respond to the Lord? We love Him, we are excited to hear His voice, but when He comes to the door, we're not sure if we want to let Him in. After all, we have our routines and they seem to be working fairly well. Why change a good thing? It's predictable, it's controllable, and it makes people happy. But what if the "good thing" isn't the highest reality God has for us? What if there is more? After a while our routines and programs become substitutes for His presence. If our programs work without Him, we continue on, and after a while we forget that Jesus is outside the door.

"The Bride of Christ has grown accustomed to living in the King's house in His absence. If she would return to the passion and hunger of her first love, she would never be content unless the King Himself were present in the house with her."[2]

The voice of the Bridegroom should awaken our hearts! When we meditate on the Word, it is the voice of the Bridegroom speaking to us. He illuminates our understanding and brings revelation. That interaction with Him causes our hearts to stir even as David's heart stirred when he wrote in Psalm 42:1–2 (NIV), "As the deer pants for streams of water, so my soul pants for you, O God. My soul thirsts for God, for the living God. When can I go and meet with God?" And the Shulamite in the Song of Solomon declared, "When I found the one my heart loves, I held him and would not let him go" (3:4 NIV).

## WHY DO WE HESITATE?

If we know Jesus is at the door and longing for us, why do we hesitate? It's not because we don't love Him; we hesitate because our love for Him is weak and immature. Often we don't understand the nature and character of the King who loves us. We have a wrong concept of God. Many people believe that God is angry with them and loves them primarily for what they can *do* for Him. They also believe that God won't really enjoy us until we die and go to heaven, where we will finally be made acceptable to Him. This wrong perception of God's character must be confronted before the church can be free to pursue the presence of Jesus with an abandoned heart.

Our lack of knowledge and revelation about the nature and character of God can cause us to back away from the Lord rather than pursue Him. If we are afraid God is angry with us, we keep our relationship with Him distant and impersonal. As a result, we reduce God to our emotional mindset, assuming He thinks the way we do, when the truth is that He doesn't. I am convinced people run from God rather than pursue Him because they aren't sure He loves them with a tender heart and longs for their fellowship.

## CHANGING OUR MOTIVATIONS

> THE LOVE OF OUR KING DEFINES OUR IDENTITY, AND THAT LOVE BECOMES OUR REALITY.

The love of our King defines our identity, and that love becomes our reality. We are created to be lovers of God. That's who we are. Everything we do for our King should flow out of this understanding of our identity. We work in His kingdom, but we do it out of abandoned hearts that are in love with Jesus. Increased intimacy with Jesus will produce a rest in our souls that protects us from frenzied ministry activity and burnout. If we are lacking in love, it's only because we have become disconnected from the source of love: Jesus. We aren't capable of loving God, ourselves, or our communities without God himself first pouring His love into our hearts.

When our hearts become protected by the knowledge that God really loves us, we don't have to perform or strive to be accepted by others. The question, especially for those of us in leadership in the church, is: What is motivating our hearts? Is it to be successful in ministry? Is it to compete with the world for the attention of people in our communities? Or is it to behold Jesus, to be conformed to His image, and to be transformed into His likeness? And do we believe that will be more effective in producing lasting fruit than our own efforts?

In Jesus we have a confidence and identity that is unshakable because we understand we are connected to something far greater than ourselves. If our security and confidence is placed in our ministry accomplishments, we will constantly try to prove our worth. This can lead to unrighteous motives and personal agendas, all in the name of God.

Success today is most often measured in terms of what we accomplish. It should be measured instead in relation to what Jesus said is first—our relationship with God. If we know we are loved, we will be able to feel God's affection, affirmation, and approval and thus be free to love Him in return. This is critical to our success in life. Once we are successful in a spiritual sense and secure in our identity, we can serve Him in ministry more effectively and with much more perseverance. We don't work in ministry to feel successful; we already know we are successful because of our relationship with Jesus. God cares deeply about our effectiveness in ministry, but it is secondary to our relationship with Him. We are called to be lovers of God first, then we will be able to effectively disciple our family, neighbors, cities, and nations.

## A HIGHER LOVE

The reality of Jesus as our Bridegroom brings delight to the human heart. When we realize how much God loves us, pursues us, and delights in us, we feel valued and spiritually confident. This revelation allows us to relate to God on the basis of intimacy. It sets our hearts free to worship Him because of who He is; it also helps us understand who *we* are. Something profound happens in our hearts when we realize that even in our immaturity, weakness, and brokenness we are desirable to God. Rather than condemning us, He is pursuing us. What a staggering concept!

God's love is not conditional like ours often is. He doesn't measure us by our performance or personal self-worth. He measures us according to the value He placed upon us when He created us and the price He paid to redeem us. In contrast, we often believe that God is only putting up with us until we get it right. So we work and work to make Him love and accept us, only to find it's not possible to work our way into His heart. When our hearts begin to respond to God out of love, we can abandon ourselves to this One who loves unconditionally. That abandonment and the ability to receive and return God's love becomes the best deterrent to sin and the best motivation to live righteously.

Understanding God's nature allows us to consider His laws and character from a place of security in our hearts. When we see Him for who He really is—in all His fullness, majesty, beauty, and perfection—the desire grows in our hearts to turn from sin and lesser things and to abandon ourselves to Him. An abandoned heart connected to the love and holiness of God is much more effective in living righteously than simply practicing "sin management."

Our first priority is our relationship with Him. Only thereafter should we be concerned about our ministry for Him. We cannot separate the first and second commandments. Love is first about loving God with all our heart and mind, then about loving our neighbors as ourselves. We must not neglect the priority of the first commandment in seeking to fulfill the second. The body of Christ will only function correctly when the first commandment is restored to first place, when our primary identity is found in Jesus, and when ministry comes as an overflow of our life in Him. This will ensure the proper expression of the second commandment.

Paul said, "Christ's love compels us" (2 Cor. 5:14 NIV). Christ's love was the driving force behind all that Paul did. Love is a much more powerful motivator than sin avoidance. What are we compelled by? Mike Bickle aptly writes in his book *The Pleasures of Loving God*: "As we position our souls to make the first commandment first, we will be lovers before we are workers. We will be worshipers before we are warriors. Through Christ's loving embrace, He will show us that we are to be a bride before we are an army."[3]

## BEING LOVED TOGETHER

When Jesus looks at a city or a community, He sees a family, those called by His name. He sees His bride and body, and His heart is toward her. He doesn't see hundreds of congregations individually; He sees one church expressed in her various flavors, cultures, and activities. Jesus is inviting us to the corporate reality of being the bride and body of Christ in our communities. When He comes to dwell in our communities, He wants to dwell in the midst of us, His entire family, household, and body, not just within our own individual expressions of His kingdom. He is our Father and He loves us together as His children. There are no favorites and yet we are each His favorite. When He comes to visit, He wants to meet with the whole family!

Not only is God interested in the family that is already called by His name, He is also vitally interested in those who have a right to the family inheritance but haven't yet heard the Good News. Cities

are very important to fulfilling God's purposes on the earth because
they are containers of many lost souls to whom He wants to bring
redemption. The ruined condition of our cities and the lost, wandering souls within them breaks His heart. We see a picture of this as
Jesus weeps over Jerusalem, saying, "How often I wanted to gather
your children together, as a hen gathers her chicks under her wings,
but you were not willing!" (Matt. 23:37).

When we as the church really comprehend the love of God and
respond to it, then our communities can also experience His love.
Cities and communities *cannot* be loved if the church doesn't understand her identity as a lover of God. The object of our affection is
the Lord; we cannot really love thousands of people we have never
met! But we can love them through the love Jesus pours out through
us. We love them because we love *Him*!

Imagine the revelation of God's love coming to the corporate
church in your community. What if everything we did was motivated
by love? Not ambition, not political agendas, not self-serving or pro-
moting, but with abandoned hearts possessed with a love that comes
from God. What if every member of God's family became a carrier
and reflector of His life, love, and presence? What might the church
look like? How much more effectively could she love and minister to
a broken community?

## Chapter 4

# THE CHURCH IN THE CITY

"THERE IS ONE BODY AND ONE SPIRIT, JUST AS
YOU WERE CALLED IN ONE HOPE OF YOUR
CALLING; ONE LORD, ONE FAITH, ONE BAPTISM;
ONE GOD AND FATHER OF ALL, WHO IS ABOVE
ALL, AND THROUGH ALL, AND IN YOU ALL."

EPHESIANS 4:4–6

God has caused His truth to be carried in many expressions throughout church history. That brings fullness to the expression of who He is. Ephesians talks about "the manifold wisdom of God" being made known by the church (Eph. 3:10). The word *manifold* describes something that is multifaceted, multicolored, like a kaleidoscope. In other words, if the church of the Lord Jesus Christ is going to be "manifold," it must include many church expressions! Just one expression of the church couldn't be considered manifold any more than the color blue could be considered the fullness of the color spectrum.

Paul shares the purpose of this in Ephesians 4:12–13, "so that the body of Christ may be built up until we all reach unity in the faith and in the knowledge of the Son of God and become mature, attaining to the whole measure of the fullness of Christ." In other words, it's time for the body of Christ to grow up!

What would that look like in your city if the corporate church "attained to the whole measure of Christ"? Would it affect how congregations related to one another or how they minister in the community?

The challenges we face in our communities won't be solved by individual efforts, no matter how impressive they may be. The devastated condition of our communities is overwhelming for any one member of the family of God. We need the presence of Jesus to be restored to His church. Citywide problems require a citywide church to cry out in desperation for the presence of God to be restored!

The body of Christ in a city is either going to be salt and light and therefore have a positive impact on the city, or the city with its opposing values will influence and mold the church into its own image. Paul connects the reality of our unity in Christ with the measure of the fullness we obtain in Him *together.* The challenge of maturity in the church is directly related to our pursuing unity in the "faith and knowledge of the Son of God."

## CORPORATE IDENTITY

The corporate reality of the body of Christ supercedes our individual identities, expressions, and cultures. Those who believe in Jesus Christ and have been saved through His death and resurrection, believing in Him for salvation, are one body, one family, and will ultimately become His bride. We are all one church under the lordship of Jesus Christ, and we should be calling people to come to Him—not to our own individual expression of the kingdom. Jesus, in John 12:32, tells us that if He is lifted up He will draw all men to *himself.*

Did you know that all but two books of our Bible are written to and for the corporate people of God? The book of Ephesians, for example, is written to the believers who lived in the city of Ephesus and was possibly circulated to other cities as well. The book of Galatians was written to the believers who lived in the cities of Galatia. In the early church, Paul and others would write letters to encourage, exhort, and disciple believers living in other cities. The letters would arrive and be read aloud publicly to the assembly of believers, who were called "the church" in that city. At that time there was not a variety of denominations; the church was one body in the city, meeting in various locations. So it was easy to communicate with the citywide church.

In the book of Revelation, Jesus writes letters to the churches in different areas of the ancient world: the church in the city of Laodicea, in Thyatira, in Philadelphia, and so on. Jesus' letters were a communication to the people of God collectively in cities; the churches were the expression of God in a particular geographical area. Even though we experience a personal or individual relationship with God through Christ Jesus, the New Testament was generally written to and for the body of Christ—the community of faith collectively or corporately. Our individualism in Western culture obscures the biblical emphasis on our corporate identity as the people of God and our relationship to our cities. Who are we as the people of God in our city?

It's obvious that things today aren't quite as simple. The corporate church has become very multidimensional and complicated. Cities have sometimes hundreds or even thousands of individual congregations. Yet the Lord still exhorts us to consider ourselves corporately by the example of the letters Jesus gives to the seven churches in the book of Revelation.

## THE BRIDE OF CHRIST IN THE CITY

The corporate church has a royal identity by virtue of being the bride of the King of Kings! God's plan for humanity from the very beginning is to prepare a beautiful bride for His perfect Son. Think about the Father's intention for His Son: to fashion out of humanity, with all its brokenness and sin, a beautiful bride for Him for eternity. The Word promises that a glorious church will be presented to Jesus "not having spot or wrinkle" (Eph. 5:27). God invites us through salvation to participate in this divine "romance." We as the church are like Ruth, who was a foreigner, an alien from another land, but was purchased by her kinsman-redeemer and became a part of the household of Israel. We are also like Esther, whose beauty won the heart of the king, and the Shulamite who was wooed by her beloved in the Song of Solomon. We are His beloved! We have been pursued, we have been redeemed, and because of the worth that He has bestowed on us, we have won the heart of our King!

When the church individually and corporately understands her true identity as the bride of Christ, she will be able to minister with greater effectiveness as she leans more and more upon Jesus. When His bride is once again rooted in His love, she will be able to comprehend with the rest of the body of Christ the love that passes knowledge and be filled with the fullness of God. We desperately need the fullness of God to come to our cities! The paltry amount we currently have is not sufficient to meet the challenges that are before us.

> For this reason I bow my knees to the Father of our Lord Jesus Christ, from whom the whole family in heaven and earth is named, that He would grant you, according to the riches of His glory, to be strengthened with might by His Spirit in the inner man, that Christ may dwell in your hearts by faith; that you, being rooted and grounded in love, may be able to comprehend with all the saints what is the breadth and length and depth and height—to know the love of Christ which passes knowledge; that you may be filled with all the fullness of God. (Ephesians 3:14–20)

What does it look like when the church is captured by the love of the King and is adorned with His beauty?

She becomes beautiful, fragrant, and attractive!

Her priorities change!

Her motivations change!

Her activities change!

Her security and confidence increase!

She becomes effective in ministry as she partners with Jesus!

## LOST SHEEP IN THE CITY

In Matthew's gospel it says that when Jesus saw the multitudes of people, He was "moved with compassion for them, because they were weary and scattered, like sheep having no shepherd" (Matt. 9:36). Having seen this, Jesus turned to His disciples and said, "The harvest truly is plentiful, but the laborers are few" (Matt. 9:37). The understanding is clear: the sheep are lost and they need a Shepherd!

Understanding the condition of the people living in our communities helps us to understand their desperate need for salvation and stirs compassion in our hearts. We cannot ignore the opportunity we have to influence our cities with the gospel. We need to look at our cities as containers filled with people, people who need Jesus.

Our cities are full of pain-filled, broken people trying to make life work for them, many of whom have no idea there is a Savior who died for them and longs for their fellowship. Our cities also contain a remnant of the community of faithful believers in Jesus Christ who have, sadly, never considered that loving the unlovable is part of their own journey of faith and destiny.

We are not only called to minister to the sheep inside the fold of the local church but also to those sheep that are still scattered in our city. Unfortunately, we spend the great bulk of our time and resources caring for the sheep that are already inside God's fold. Jesus says in John 10 that He is the Good Shepherd and "the good shepherd gives His life for the sheep." We must have the same heart, concerned about ministering to the people in our communities.

Many times we pray "long distance" for people, from our comfort zone, never connecting with them in a tangible way. We are trying to minister to the people in our city without any direct contact!

WE CANNOT MINISTER WITHOUT HUMAN CONTACT! KINGDOM MINISTRY IS A "FULL CONTACT" ACTIVITY!

When Jesus said to His new disciples, "Follow Me," where did He lead them? It was to broken, hurting people. The disciples didn't want to do that at first; they didn't understand that Jesus had come to love, to serve, and then to die for them. We see several examples where they were indignant (Mark 6:37); they rebuked people Jesus was trying to minister to (Mark 10:13–14), and they were concerned with achieving a place of importance in the ministry with Jesus (Mark 9:34).

The picture of the disciples that we see in the Gospels is in sharp contrast to the one we see in the Epistles! The work of the Cross in their lives and the power that came from the Holy Spirit on the Day of Pentecost turned these disciples into radical, effective leaders who sacrificed themselves to build the kingdom of God and minister the life of Jesus to people in many different cities.

We must learn the same lessons the disciples learned from walking with Jesus. His ministry is about touching people, healing the sick, feeding the poor, and saving the lost. We cannot minister without human contact! Kingdom ministry is a "full contact" activity!

## UNDERSTANDING THE CONDITION OF THE LOST

God intends that our cities be places of refuge and shelter for the people who live there. Whether that is true or not depends upon the condition of the church and how effective she is in meeting the needs of the lost sheep in the city.

People living in our society can feel disconnected, isolated, and alone, even in the midst of nonstop commercialism and busyness. Being surrounded by relentless activity causes tremendous stress and anxiety, and high turnover in the marketplace can cause people to feel used. Our world today is moving so fast that it's almost exclusively temporally focused, and relationships are consistently broken because no one has the time to invest in them.

People typically don't admit they struggle with such feelings, because they are generally unaware of these deeper root issues. But you can see the fruit of these issues in outward expressions and behavior. For instance, we see the casual and illicit sexual behavior people engage in to numb their loneliness and rejection and the expressions of violence in which they attempt to regain control. Workplace corruption often occurs because people feel they are entitled to exact their own justice.

In his book *Taking Our Cities for God* John Dawson shares that people who live in cities often become idolaters, participating in whatever the city offers them. People can find counterfeits of God's kingdom where they live, work, and play. Satan counterfeits the work of the Holy Spirit in the form of false religion, while sports figures, celebrities, and political leaders become "heroes" and replace the role of the Lord Jesus as the Son of God. And God the Father is replaced by large institutions and corporations.[1]

While cities are supposedly developed for the benefit of the people living there, they can begin to feel like victims of institutions and structures rather than beneficiaries of them. "Because of the disorientation they experience, urban dwellers are extremely vulnerable to both sweeping revival and mass deception through some false hope."[2]

## JESUS—THE GREAT REFORMER!

We can't possibly solve the overwhelming situations facing our cities today with mere human wisdom and programs. Social reform and political legislation, while offering some relief, cannot begin to resolve the multitude of problems facing society today. We can offer assistance, but the root causes for what ails society are spiritual issues. How do you solve the divorce rate? the suicide rate? the illegitimate birth rate? We cannot cure corruption or hatred, we cannot protect innocent people from terrorists willing to die for their cause, and we cannot put bandages on the symptoms of serious spiritual disease. We must address root issues that cause people to hate, not to value life, to steal, to live an immoral lifestyle. Social reform is necessary and helpful to a degree, but having the great Reformer in our midst is much more effective!

When Jesus began His public ministry, He announced His purpose by quoting Isaiah 61:1–2:

> "The Spirit of the Lord is upon Me, because He has anointed Me to preach the gospel to the poor; He has sent Me to heal the brokenhearted, to proclaim liberty to the captives and recovery of sight to the blind, to set at liberty those who are oppressed; to proclaim the acceptable year of the Lord" (Luke 4:18–19).

He left all the glory of heaven and put on a human body for thirty-three years. He subjected himself to natural laws of hunger, fatigue, and human emotions. He lived here! He walked through communities and demonstrated His love and power to people in tangible ways. Wherever Jesus went, the blind were healed, the demons were terrified, the lame walked, and the demonically oppressed were set free. Huge crowds followed Him, listening, watching, and waiting to see what He would do. Who would He heal? When Jesus stepped foot in a community, things changed!

The ministry of Jesus hasn't changed. When Jesus is invited into a community, He brings life and powerful transformation.

## EARLY CHURCH

After Jesus left the earth, His influence and the work of the Holy Spirit was evident in the life of the early church. In Acts 2, it is recorded that the believers lived simple but faithful lives, sharing their possessions, listening to teaching, fellowshipping, and praying together. The results of this lifestyle of faithful devotion were powerful. In verse 43, it says, "Fear came upon every soul and many wonders and signs were done through the apostles." Throughout the book of Acts and the Epistles, the church of the Lord Jesus walked in great authority, power, and victory over the enemy.

There is a stunning parallel in Acts regarding the simplicity of the lives of the believers and the power and effectiveness of their ministry. They didn't have complicated strategies or programs; they had the authority of Christ and the power of the Holy Spirit. Their lives had been turned upside down by their encounter with Jesus; they loved Him! They abandoned themselves to serving His kingdom; they persevered, they suffered, they ministered with power, and they impacted their cities.

They didn't need revival because they were living in the overflow of the original outpouring of the Holy Spirit's presence and power. The purpose of revival now is to restore the church back to her original state of righteousness, authority, purpose, and power.

Jesus says in the gospel of Luke, "I must preach the kingdom of God to the other cities also, because for this purpose I have been sent" (Luke 4:43). Jesus came to the earth to purchase our redemption and to empower us to take that good news to the rest of the world.

The only real hope for the world today is that the manifest presence of Jesus, and therefore His love and power, be restored to His church; then she can become a tangible reality in our communities. We need the presence of the King to come with His mercy, compassion, healing, and delivering power!

## PROMISES OF RESTORATION

The Great Commission began with a city (Jerusalem) and will end with a city (the New Jerusalem). God has made it clear in His Word that we as His body are commissioned to partner with Him in the rebuilding of devastated places like our cities. Part of the mandate of the gospel is to reach the multitudes with the transforming power of Jesus Christ that in turn makes it possible to restore and rebuild cities spiritually, morally, and socially.

Scripture is full of prophetic promises that "places long devastated" will be rebuilt, that springs will burst forth in the desert places, that wastelands will be renewed. God really means that, and He means it for your city as well. (See Isaiah 32:1, 15, 18; 35:1–2, 6–7; 41:18, 20; 43:18–19; 44:3–4; 58:12.)

Isaiah 61:4 promises that "they shall rebuild the old ruins, they shall raise up the former desolations, and they shall repair the ruined cities, the desolations of many generations." It goes on to say, "Instead

of your shame you shall have double honor, and instead of confusion
they shall rejoice in their portion. Therefore in their land they shall
possess double; everlasting joy shall be theirs" (Isa. 61:7).

## THE IMPACT OF A DESPERATE CITYWIDE CHURCH

A good illustration of the powerful impact of Jesus through His
body on behalf of a devastated community is the testimony of Almolonga, Guatemala. Featured on the first *Transformation* video, Almolonga has become a powerful example of God's transforming power
and one of the most thorough transformation testimonies in the
world. When Jesus stepped into this community, He impacted not
only the church but every sphere of society as well.

George Otis Jr. documents this testimony in his book *Informed
Intercession*:

The town of Almolonga was typical of Mayan communities,
plagued with addiction to alcohol, steeped in idolatry, and poverty-
stricken. The people who were full of fear and seeking relief from
their poverty looked for support in alcohol and a local idol named
Maximon. Tired of living under the influence of idolatry, a group of
believers began crying out to God during evening prayer vigils
beginning in August 1974. They gathered together in unity and
declared freedom over their community. They resisted the enemy in
their midst and the devastating consequences of his presence among
them. In the months that followed many people were delivered by
the power of God! God began to respond to their faith and prayer,
delivering many who were demonically oppressed and physically
afflicted. As a result, many committed their lives to Christ.

After God began to visit the land, an unprecedented revival
occurred. Families were touched and transformed by the power of
God. Miracles of healing and deliverance have caused the city to be
called both the "City of Miracles" and the "City of God." Today
more than 90 percent of the people in the community have become
evangelical Christians, and there are nearly two dozen evangelical
churches. The life of the community, the families, agriculture, businesses, center around the life of the church.[3]

Local people refer to their community in terms of two time frames:
*before* the power of God came, and *after* He came! When the presence
of Jesus became a tangible reality in the community, He brought life

and restoration to "places long devastated" (Isa. 61:4). The last jail closed in Almolonga nine years ago. Imagine, children are growing up without any concept of crime or violence in their community!

Many of the businesses in town have also been named after the faith of the people. For refreshments and a quick snack, you can step into the "Store of Angels" or "The Shop of Hope." If you are not feeling well, visit the "Bethany Pharmacy" or "Adonia Medicines." Hungry? Stop in the "Canaan Bakery" or "Store of Bethany." If you need some work done on your car, you can take it to the "Jehovah-Jireh Auto Repair" or "Christ Metal Works." If you need to buy a new dress, just visit "God's Textured Cloth" or the "Genesis Boutique."

Not only did the Lord save and heal the people, He also healed the land! Today Almolonga produces the largest and best vegetables in that part of the world, which has caused Almolonga to also be known as "America's vegetable garden." They are producing several harvests per year; growing cycles have shortened, and they are providing produce for many neighboring communities and countries as well.

On a recent trip, I visited the "Hall of Fame," a large building in the middle of town that is used for the vegetable market. I could barely hold a cabbage in one arm and a green onion in the other! The cabbage was several feet wide, carrots were twice the size of my arm, and the celery was over three feet in length! It wasn't the size of the vegetables that impressed us as much as the great abundance of them. We visited the market on a Saturday *after* more than sixty trucks had left with all their loads for the day, and the leftover amount was staggering. Vegetables were piled in stacks several feet high, filling a room the size of a square block! Not only are the vegetables supernaturally large and in great abundance, they are vibrant in color and taste delicious. I asked a pastor if these vegetables have contributed to the health of the people in the city, and he said yes; they only pray for two or three sick people a month in a church of one thousand people.

On almost every vehicle you see drive through the community, there are bold stickers making statements of faith: "Gift of God Toyota," "Jehovah-Nissi," "Jesus Is My King," "Jesus Christ Truck," "Humble Servant Toyota," and "Truck of Faith."

The most amazing indication of the transformation of the community is that the glory of God is evident in the lives of the people.

Families are restored and more—their smiles, the obvious joy and peace that saturates the city is hard to describe. This is truly a place where the heavens are open and Jesus is being glorified in every aspect of life!

As you enter Almolonga, you are welcomed by a large banner hung across the main street. It reads in big bold print: "Jesus is Lord over Almolonga." Indeed!

It is truly amazing to visit Almolonga, because you not only sense the tangible presence of the Lord dwelling in the land, you can also actually see the effect of the gospel! Isn't that what we want for our communities?

## GOD'S GLORY SPREADS!

Almolonga is not alone in this amazing transformation, according to The Sentinel Group. While they had identified only eight transformed communities in 1998, today there are over two hundred communities experiencing God's transforming power in the world. Some of these are large cities, some are small villages up in the mountains; God's glory is spreading everywhere. People with their hearts stirred by faith are pressing into God to see His divine purposes fulfilled in their own communities. There is evidence of an amazing acceleration going on in the kingdom of God. Revival is beginning on a broad scale and is impacting communities like we have never seen before.

The reports of God's work in these communities are stunning. Suicide rates are plummeting, jails are closing, barren land is springing back to life, political and social structures are being turned upside down. The citywide church is fasting, praying, and worshiping together—and God is being glorified!

# DOOR OF HOPE

"BEHOLD, I WILL ALLURE HER, [I] WILL BRING
HER INTO THE WILDERNESS, AND SPEAK
COMFORT TO HER. I WILL GIVE HER HER
VINEYARDS FROM THERE AND THE VALLEY OF
ACHOR [TROUBLE] AS A DOOR OF HOPE; SHE
SHALL SING THERE, AS IN THE DAYS OF HER
YOUTH, AS IN THE DAY WHEN SHE CAME UP
FROM THE LAND OF EGYPT."

HOSEA 2:14-15

## Chapter 5

# GOD:
# PRESENT OR ABSENT?

"No longer will they call you Deserted,
or name your land Desolate."

Isaiah 62:4 niv

If God's presence is required for transformation, then we must ask the question, "Is God's presence present?" We face a sobering fact: Although many communities in the world are undergoing spiritual transformation, none of them is located in the Western world. I don't know about you, but I want to know why. Why isn't the Lord coming to inhabit our cities? Where *is* Jesus?

Whenever you suggest the need for God's presence in our cities, interesting conversations result. That topic raises implications some people don't like. I have had people demand to know if I were suggesting Jesus *isn't* present in His church in the city, and whether I understood that the church *is* the temple of God. The implication is that if there is a church in the city, obviously God is dwelling in it! In other words, if we build it, He will come. But is that true?

I have pondered these objections deeply. While I do agree that God intends that the church be the temple of His presence in a city, is it a *present* reality? To what kind of church is the Lord making His promises? The Bible teaches that the manifest presence of the Lord is directly linked to righteousness and holiness (Revelation 3:14–22) and that the church's authority and effectiveness is directly related to

her unity (John 17). When the corporate church in a city is fragmented, full of sin, confused, and compromising with the spirit of
this world, how much demonstration of the Holy Spirit's presence
are we biblically justified to expect? How much impact on our cities
and communities may be reasonably expected in our present state?

There cannot be restoration without presence or redemption
without an intimate encounter with God. Without the presence of
Jesus dwelling in the land, we have no hope. While there are countless opinions regarding the challenges before the church and just as
many suggestions about how to remedy our situation, very few of
those discussions indicate concern about the lack of the manifest
presence of the Lord in His temple.

## UNDERSTANDING OUR CONDITION

We cannot change something until we understand its true condition, and we cannot change something we don't love and are not
willing to sacrifice for.

A good example of this in Scripture is the report Nehemiah
received of the devastated condition of the city of Jerusalem. When
Nehemiah heard the troubling report: "The survivors who are left
from the captivity in the province are there in great distress and
reproach. The wall of Jerusalem is also broken down, and its gates are
burned with fire" (Neh. 1:3), it broke his heart. He began to cry out
to God on behalf of the city he loved: "So it was, when I heard these
words, that I sat down and wept, and mourned for many days; I was
fasting and praying before the God of heaven" (Neh. 1:4).

But Nehemiah didn't only pray, he became the answer to his own
prayers for restoration. He returned to Jerusalem to lead the transformation effort of the city. Similarly, there isn't an alien army that's
going to come down from another planet and change our communities! God wants to bring restoration through His body, the church.
If our communities are going to be transformed, it will be as a result
of our prayer and our labor with God to bring it to pass. This isn't
merely a nice spiritual sentiment; it will require sacrifice, time,
resources, commitment, and responsibility.

When the believers in Jesus Christ are living in a city that has
been devastated and ruined—morally, spiritually, economically, and
socially—we are perceived by the world as anything but victorious.

Instead, we Christians are often pitied and viewed as irrelevant to the culture around us. When the church looks like a "hostage" in the midst of destruction and darkness around us, how is that glorifying to the Lord?

The Lord showed me something once in the natural that I felt was a good analogy of what was happening in the spiritual. It was during a drive through the inner city of Los Angeles. I was grieving over the ruined condition of the neighborhoods. Block after block of destroyed buildings, burned with fire and abandoned, children wandering in the streets, gangs and violence evident everywhere. But on every block there was also a small church. At first I felt hopeful that the people of God were present and had established a congregation in the midst of the devastation. But then I looked closer and saw that these small churches were covered with graffiti and black iron bars covered the doors and windows.

Then I noticed the names of the churches: the "most" of this or the "first" of that. Sometimes the name of the church stretched all the way across the top of the building! I couldn't help but see the irony of what the church was calling herself versus the obvious reality that closed in tighter and tighter as the ruins of the neighborhood pressed in. I visited some of those churches, and I attended one regularly. While the faith and life that existed among the people was deep and real, clearly they were in a defensive posture and not a victorious one in relationship to their impact on the community around them.

> WHEN THE CHURCH LOOKS LIKE A "HOSTAGE" IN THE MIDST OF DESTRUCTION AND DARKNESS AROUND US, HOW IS THAT GLORIFYING TO THE LORD?

The church I attended was a product of the Azusa Street Revival in 1906 and was located just down the street from the original location where God poured out His Spirit in a way that eventually spread around the world. The walls of the church were covered with old photos of the revival, hundreds of people standing together year after year as the revival spread and grew. Crutches and other things were hanging on the walls, silently testifying to the power of God that had healed so many—in the good old days, when God came. About twenty people still attended that big old church when I was there, but the days of the visitation of His presence were clearly over.

This isn't true only of congregations in the inner city. The ruined condition may be more noticeable there, but what about the suburbs? The pristine appearance of our suburbs hides just as much sin and devastation. That's where most churches are moving today, trying to escape the ruins of the inner city, moving out to where it's quieter, safer, and more pleasant. After all, the people in the suburbs need Jesus too, we argue. While that is true, oftentimes our new church projects continue to reflect our defeat at being an agent of change in our communities and our fear of the darkness that is closing in on us.

Jesus is coming back for a victorious church! He isn't coming back to a broken, defeated, irrelevant one. What kind of a bride would that make for God's perfect Son?

When we see the ruined condition of our cities and communities, it should break our hearts and stir us to prayer. We have underestimated the pain in God's heart over the devastation and brokenness of people who live in darkness. Isaiah 9:2 declares what the result would be when Jesus' presence came to earth: "The people walking in darkness have seen a great light" (NIV). God fully intends to continue to bring hope and restoration to forsaken, desolate communities, and He is looking for those who will partner with Him.

What is the report of *your* city? How many lost people live in it? How many orphaned children? Are there suicides? People being murdered or raped? How many? How many die from disease or suffer from loneliness? What about the civil government: is there corruption? And the church: are there scandals, divisions, or self-promotion?

> For the Lord brings a charge against the inhabitants of the land: There is no truth or mercy or knowledge of God in the land. By swearing and lying, killing and stealing and committing adultery, they break all restraint, with bloodshed upon bloodshed. Therefore the land will mourn; and everyone who dwells there will waste away. (Hosea 4:1–3)

It's *not* okay that our cities are being handed over to the enemy without contest by the body of Christ. There isn't anything in the Bible that says the people of God are supposed to live in a defensive posture in the midst of wickedness! Quite the contrary; aren't we called to be "overcomers"? (See 1 John 2:13; Revelation 12:11.) We haven't yet realized the consequences of our lack of unity and refusal to contend for God's presence. I want to encourage you to consider the condition of your city: Watch the news, read the newspaper, listen to conversations, and look at the people around you. Let the condition of your city break your heart and draw you into intercession for a breakthrough of God's presence.

## CAUSES FOR BARRENNESS

The church in the Western world is not barren because of a lack of activities. Ministries are abounding and flourishing. Never in history have we had so many creative expressions of the church reaching out to people in their communities. At the same

> THE ONLY SOLUTION TO BARRENNESS IS PRESENCE.

time we find ourselves struggling to be a relevant influence on our culture. Society may appreciate our help at times, but it doesn't want our counsel. And despite more effort than ever to appear relevant, never has the church been more irrelevant to the world around us. The church is viewed as simply another option, part of the spiritual smorgasbord on the religious table. While many people find *comfort within* the church, they aren't looking for *direction from* the church.

The gap between the church and the people of a city that don't know Jesus has grown so wide, we have all but lost our ability to span it. Although we are attempting to build bridges, it's like throwing a rope ladder across the Grand Canyon—it just won't work. We must be willing to evaluate why we have lost influence in society. We need to look at ourselves first and ask God to give us insight about our own condition before we attempt to change our surroundings. The truth is the world doesn't *want* our religion. It isn't interested in our church culture or becoming one of our statistics. But many people will respond to God's love genuinely expressed through His people who carry the fragrance of Christ.

The Western church is busy working hard for God, while the Lord is longing for her fellowship. Even the most spiritual activities have fallen into the ever-increasing pot of excuses for the lack of God's presence. Take prayer, for instance. It's amazing how much time we believers spend talking about prayer, reading about prayer, and holding conferences about prayer. Yet never have we been so preoccupied and infiltrated by worldliness. How much time do we actually spend praying?

The church is very busy, but our activities aren't necessarily producing new disciples. There has been almost no change in the percentage of people who call themselves Christian or who regularly attend church in the last two decades. What's interesting is that the American church has raised and spent over $1 trillion on domestic ministry without producing a measurable increase in the church's primary purpose: leading people to Christ and making disciples.[1] Our spiritual barrenness won't be resolved with more programs or human ingenuity. The only solution to barrenness is presence.

## HIS PRESENCE—WITHDRAWING OR RETURNING?

Have you ever wondered if it is possible to get God's attention or attract His presence? And if it is possible, then why don't we spend more time doing those things that welcome His presence? God's Word establishes clear principles regarding His presence. There are things that prepare for and welcome the presence of the Lord—things like prayer, unity, worship, and a broken and contrite spirit. There are also things that cause Him to withdraw or remain at a distance. God makes it clear in 2 Chronicles that it *is* possible to gain His favor and attention. Look what He says to Solomon after the dedication of the temple:

> Then the Lord appeared to Solomon by night, and said to him: "I have heard your prayer, and have chosen this place for Myself as a house of sacrifice. When I shut up heaven and there is no rain, or command the locusts to devour the land, or send pestilence among My people, if My people who are called by My name will humble themselves, and pray and seek My face, and turn from their wicked ways, then I will hear from heaven, and will forgive their sin and heal their land" (2 Chronicles 7:12–14).

These verses summarize the covenant agreement God made with His people. The covenant clearly identifies responsibilities of the people (to humble themselves, pray, seek His face, and turn from

their wicked ways) and of God (to hear, forgive, and heal their land).
In other words, God would fulfill His part of the covenant if they
fulfilled theirs!

Then the Lord continues and says something amazing:

> Now My eyes will be open and My ears attentive to prayer
> made in this place. For now I have chosen and sanctified this house,
> that My name may be there forever; and My eyes and My heart will
> be there perpetually. (2 Chronicles 7:15–16)

Why "now"? What had just taken place that caused the Lord to give the people His attention? The restored covenant! Solomon prepared the house of the Lord and the people of God to be a place where God could "rest" and dwell among them.

> THE MOST NOBLE THING A HUMAN BEING CAN DO IS BECOME A LIGHTNING ROD FOR GOD'S PRESENCE IN HIS OR HER COMMUNITY.

Imagine God saying that to your community—that His eyes and ears are open and that He has chosen you to be a "house of sacrifice," that His name and heart would be with you forever!

The most noble thing a human being can do is become a lightning rod for God's presence in his or her community.

## HINDRANCES FOR GOD'S PRESENCE

What are some of the things that hinder God's presence from being manifest in our midst? While this is by no means a comprehensive list, I want to highlight the most prevalent issues that can keep the Lord's presence at a distance.

### *Idolatry*

The Lord's presence can be drawn and welcomed to a place but it can also be driven away. Ezekiel warns that any kind of idolatry encroaches on God's glory and brings reproach to His name. For example, in Ezekiel 8–11, God's presence left the temple *because* of the leaders' idolatry. This isn't an example of a *lack* of God's presence but rather of God making a deliberate *choice* to withdraw:

> He said to me, "Son of man, do you see what they are doing,
> the great abominations that the house of Israel commits here, to

make Me go far away from My sanctuary? . . . Have you seen what the elders of the house of Israel do in the dark, every man in the room of his idols? For they say, 'The Lord does not see us, the Lord has forsaken the land.' Is it a trivial thing to the house of Judah to commit the abominations which they commit here? For they have filled the land with violence; then they have returned to provoke Me to anger. . . . Therefore I also will act in fury. My eye will not spare nor will I have pity; and though they cry in My ears with a loud voice, I will not hear them" (Ezekiel 8:6, 12, 17–18).

The temple leaders were actually worshiping the sun god *inside* the temple! Talk about blatant idolatry! Their idolatry resulted in the Lord's turning away from them and saying He would not hear them. God withdrew His glory first from the temple and then from the city. The Lord didn't point out the sin in the city first or hold the city responsible for the withdrawing of His glory. He held the people of God responsible, and their idolatry led to the city losing His presence and the blessings that went with it.

Paul says in 2 Corinthians 6:16–17:

And what agreement has the temple of God with idols? For you are the temple of the living God. As God has said: "I will dwell in them and walk among them. I will be their God and they shall be My people." Therefore "come out from among them and be separate," says the Lord. "Do not touch what is unclean, And I will receive you."

One interesting fact in the Ezekiel passage is that the leaders of God's house excused their idolatry by saying, "The Lord doesn't see us for God has forsaken the land" (Ezek. 8:12). They blamed God and failed to see the consequences their own sin had caused in the city. What a sobering reality that God could slowly withdraw His presence from His sanctuary and that it could go unnoticed by those ministering and worshiping there! As a result, God says *His ears will no longer hear the cry of the people in the city*. Idolatry erects a wall that separates us from the presence of the Lord. God won't cross it because He won't add His glory to our idolatry.

I doubt if there is much "sun god" worship going on in our services, but there is certainly a good measure of idolatry, nonetheless.

Anything that competes for our love of Jesus can become a substitute for our affections and worship. George Barna reports: "The average congregant spends more time watching television in *one day* than he spends in all spiritual pursuits combined for an *entire week*."[2] Where are we spending our time? our money? our affections?

Psalm 24:3–4 states: "Who may ascend into the hill of the Lord? Or who may stand in His holy place? He who has clean hands and a pure heart, who has not lifted up his soul to an idol, nor sworn deceitfully."

The Lord is inviting us to ascend His holy hill and fellowship with Him, but sin has cause-and-effect consequences that keep the Lord at a distance. This can happen on a personal level or a corporate level. When we lose our perceptible sense of His presence, we conclude, "God doesn't see or hear us." We go about our own business and stop expecting His presence. The church may talk about the day God will come and pour out revival; some people may talk about the "good old days" when God came. But where is the present-tense reality of His manifest presence?

### Immorality

The church in recent years has been riddled with accusations of immorality among leaders. Hardly a day goes by that we don't hear a charge of sexual abuse, corruption, or moral failure among members of the clergy. The Lord is exposing our sin, just as the prophet Hosea warned: "I will uncover her lewdness in the sight of her lovers" (Hos. 2:10).

The immorality of the church has weakened our authority to speak about issues of morality, honesty, and trust. Why should the world believe our message? As of this writing, there is a debate underway to make an amendment to our constitution to define marriage as between a man and a woman! We are living in a moral war zone and the enemy has taken off his gloves. Churches are being split down the middle over basic tenets of faith; some are simply rewriting the tenets to suit their compromised position on morality.

Some of the church's immoral condition is now "legitimized" by new legislation. An example of that is the recent decision by the Episcopal Church, which led to the ordination of a homosexual bishop. During the debate leading up to the decision, Gene Robinson commented to the Associated Press that he considered his relationship with his gay partner "sacramental."[3] *Sacramental?* How can something God calls "abominable" now be viewed as sacred? The answer is that idolatry and apostasy result in spiritual darkness and deception. What in the world is going on? And how can it be going on *inside* the church at the altars where we are to seek God and ask for forgiveness of sin?

Of great concern is how the church responds to the immorality in our culture. There is very little identification with sin, as was demonstrated by Nehemiah and Daniel. If there is repentance, it is in general terms. The church tries to protect herself by focusing on the sin "out there"—so it doesn't get "inside."

What we fail to understand is that the sin is already "inside"—that's the problem! The evidence indicates that most sin that goes on "out there" is also being committed within the church. According to biblical principle, then, until we cleanse the temple inside we have no authority to address or influence what's happening outside the church. When the church protests against immorality, and then immorality is found within her walls, it gives the enemy and the world every opportunity to accuse us of being hypocrites.

When the church processes sin issues internally, through desperate prayer, repentance, and turning back to holiness, the fruit of that work is revival. When the revived church begins to influence society externally, then we will see results in community transformation.

## Ambition and Independence

God wants to dwell in the midst of His unified church. But the church is still struggling to walk in unity. We may say yes to citywide unity in the body of Christ, but for the most part we haven't figured out how to make that a reality in practice. We must (1) learn how to value the various parts of the body in their own unique functions; and (2) understand how we fit together for the sake of demonstrating the manifold wisdom of God through His body, thereby bringing life and hope to our city.

The more determined we are to remain independent, the more excuses we will find not to function in unity with the rest of the body. Oftentimes these excuses sound spiritual, and we all use them. I have heard many leaders say things like "They [other leaders] don't share my vision or revelation" or "God has called me/my church to reach the city." Of course He has! He has called *all* of us to that task; it's not unique to whoever hears it first! The complaint often expressed by leaders is "I can't wait for other leaders to get the vision." My question is "What has impatience gained us?" God's purposes aren't intended to work in isolation from the corporate reality of God's family. Why would God validate our ministry with fruitfulness when we are violating His expressed principles regarding unity?

I am not suggesting that we find unity at the lowest common denominator, thereby watering everything down until there is no vision or anointing left. I am talking about finding our unity at the highest level—around the throne of God—and being willing to build together according to the purposes of God.

Because we aren't hearing God *together* in prayer, we sense what He is saying individually and then assume that we must work out the vision we receive *individually*. That is an erroneous conclusion. God doesn't intend for us to accomplish corporate purposes without corporate agreement and unity. It's not possible to have a lasting corporate impact on a city as a single congregation. God hasn't constructed the rules of life that way. It requires corporate unity and agreement to accomplish corporate results.

We as individuals can exercise authority and responsibility for ourselves. If we are a spouse or a parent, we have spiritual authority and responsibility for our spouse and/or our children. If we are responsible for a department in our workplace, we have been given responsibility to administrate that department. But only the church, the body and bride of Christ, is given dominion over whole cities and territories. Think of the analogy of the body that Paul refers to in 1 Corinthians 12 and Ephesians 4; it would be ludicrous for the knee to declare it had authority over the entire body! And so is the local pastor or leader out of line who declares that he will reach his city or community by himself.

God has ordained a corporate church in each city! There is something bigger than our local congregations! There should be one Shepherd and one King enthroned in our cities. We must start with a common vision and purpose and then build according to God's blueprint, not our own. We can't start with our own empire and then try to build up to who God is. He will step down to us in response to our desperate cry.

Psalm 133 promises us that when we "dwell together in unity," our unity becomes like oil, and in that place of unity the Lord commands His blessing and presence.

## The Spirit of Unbelief

Another challenge we face is "having a form of godliness but denying its power" (2 Tim. 3:5). We are handcuffed to the spirit of unbelief! I'm not talking about simply having a lack of faith. A lack of faith sounds like we're just missing something, but the situation is much more serious than that! Unbelief is like a heavy blanket cloaking the church, suffocating the life out of her. Unbelief is denial of God's nature and His promises. This hardening of our hearts ultimately causes us to miss God's intended purposes for us.

A good example of this is when the Israelites approached the Promised Land. Moses sent in spies to look for several things, including whether the land was good or bad and to bring back some of its fruit. The spies went in and brought back grapes so large two men were required to carry one cluster! They reported that indeed it was a good land flowing with milk and honey. But then they reported something else: "Nevertheless the people who dwell in the land are strong, the cities are fortified and very large; moreover we saw the descendants of Anak there" (Num. 13:28). Their report about "giants" in the land caused quite a stir.

Most of the spies were full of fear and unbelief. As a result, the people concluded it would be better to return to Egypt or to die in the wilderness. One and a half years after their miraculous deliverance from Egypt, the people decided that returning to bondage under Pharaoh was more appealing then facing some giants with God! When Joshua and Caleb exhorted the people to trust God for the land He had brought them to the people tried to stone them. Seeing their unbelief God wanted to destroy the people, but Moses interceded again for the sake of the people and convinced God to spare their lives. When God relented, He gave this as His reason for relenting: "But My servant Caleb, *because he has a different spirit in him* and has followed Me fully, I will bring into the land where he went and his descendants shall inherit it" (Num. 14:24, emphasis added).

The story doesn't end there. God proceeded to judge the spies who had "gathered together against Me" and said they would die in the wilderness. Just as they requested! Here is the death sentence:

> Now the men whom Moses sent to spy out the land, who returned and made all the congregation complain against him *by bringing a bad report of the land,* those very men who brought the evil report about the land died by the plague before the Lord. (Numbers 14:36–37, emphasis added)

God destroyed them not because they were afraid of the giants but because they *rebelled against the land God had brought them to and gave a bad report to the people*!

All but two of the spies saw the giants in the land, calculated their ability to meet the challenge, and shrunk back in fear and unbelief. Joshua and Caleb saw the same giants but they also recognized the land of promise as from God. Therefore, their calculations included God going before them into the land of promise. God went before Israel into the land and led them to victory after victory, supernaturally moving on their behalf.

We can't defeat giants on our own. God never asks us to, but we must agree with God's promises and purposes and walk in faith that *He* will accomplish them.

What report do we bring about the land God has brought us to? What do we believe about it? Do we have a "different" spirit like Caleb, or are we part of the unbelieving, complaining congregation gathered against God regarding the land? Which spirit is permeating the church in the Western world—that of the people filled with unbelief, or that of Caleb and Joshua?

Have you ever wondered why miracles happen so easily in non-Western nations? Why does revival and evangelism seem so easy in other places? From my experience, I believe the primary reason for this is the issue of faith versus unbelief.

Jesus promised us some amazing things: "Most assuredly, I say to you, he who believes in Me, the works that I do he will do also; and greater works than these he will do because I go to My Father" (John 14:12) and "Whatever you ask in My name, that I will do, that the Father may be glorified in the Son. If you ask anything in My name,

I will do it" (John 14:13–14). It seems there are believers that walk
in faith according to God's Word and actually see it worked out in
their everyday lives. Then there are those of us who believe it intel-
lectually but rarely see it accomplished.

What is God asking us to enter into? Do we have faith for it?
Once we have been influenced by a spirit of unbelief, it works its
way into every part of our life of faith.

We must agree with God's promises for our lives and for our
communities and root out the unbelief that hinders us from entering
into the fullness He has for us and the people to which we are called
to minister. We must become like Caleb—people with a "different
spirit"!

### Harlotry

The curious thing about the bride of Christ is how prone she is
to wander away from the One to whom she is betrothed! It's amazing
to me how clearly God has expressed His love for us, ultimately sending His own Son into the world to save and redeem us, and yet we
still wander away.

It seems that after living the Christian life for a while, our true
identity as a bride becomes cloudy and we wander away from intimacy with Christ. That's when we become so easily preoccupied
with distracting activities which eventually leads to spiritual harlotry.
The church is preoccupied with other interests, and many of the
things she loves are of the world. A Laodicean-type church results
from being infiltrated by a worldly culture.

When the church doesn't know the love of her King, she turns
to other lovers. She always has. Spiritual adultery is a recurring theme
in the Word of God. It was the ongoing issue between the Lord and
Israel. Who would they love? Who would they worship? We could
ask ourselves the same questions. Has the church left her first love?
Has she been pursuing things of the world? Here is the rebuke that
Jesus gave to the church at Ephesus in the second chapter of Revelation:

> "I know your works, your labor, your patience, and that you
> cannot bear those who are evil. And you have tested those who say
> they are apostles and are not, and have found them liars; and you

have persevered and have patience, and have labored for My name's sake and have not become weary. Nevertheless I have this against you, that you have left your first love. Remember therefore from where you have fallen; repent and do the first works, or else I will come to you quickly and remove your lampstand from its place—unless you repent" (Revelation 2:2–5).

The church has lost her fascination with the person of Jesus Christ and has become fascinated with the things of the world. We can't hope to see revival or city transformation before the individual hearts of God's people return to Him. In the book of Ezekiel, for instance, the Lord is speaking of His love for Jerusalem but also of her harlotry. She took the precious things He gave her and used them for her harlotry:

> "But you trusted in your own beauty, played the harlot because of your fame, and poured out your harlotry on everyone passing by who would have it. . . . You have also taken your beautiful jewelry from My gold and My silver, which I had given you, and made for yourself male images and played the harlot with them" (Ezekiel 16:15, 17–18).

And in Hosea:

> "For she did not know that I gave her grain, new wine, and oil, and multiplied her silver and gold—which they prepared for Baal. . . . I will punish her for the days of the Baals to which she burned incense. She decked herself with her earrings and jewelry, and went after her lovers; but Me she forgot," says the Lord. (Hosea 2:8, 13)

What is the Lord saying in these passages? He is saying that the beautiful things she possessed actually came from Him and still belong to Him, but now she is using them in her pursuit of other lovers. That is harlotry. Are we offering our beauty to the god of this world? Who does our beauty belong to? Whose attention and approval are we seeking?

The Lord adorns us with His love and beauty, but He doesn't want that adornment to be used for other lovers. *While the church's beauty will be seen and enjoyed by many, it is to be offered to Him alone.*

The spirit of harlotry *must* come out of the bride! The book of Revelation describes two corporate women. The first woman is described as a "great harlot" (Rev. 17:1) and represents compromised religion at the end of the age that Satan uses to help further the political goals of the Antichrist. In contrast to the great harlot is the chaste, pure bride of Christ, who is given wholly to her Bridegroom (Revelation 19:7–8).

## Self-Righteousness

Unfortunately, one of our most serious offenses is our self-righteousness and pride. What is the response of the church to the condition of the city? We have either totally ignored the ruined condition of the city or blamed others for her desolation. For too long the church has abdicated her spiritual authority, choosing to rely on secular, social institutions to meet the needs of the people. But who has been given the moral and spiritual authority in a city? The police department? The state welfare system? No!

The people of God are meant to influence the city through every institution. Jesus said that we are to be "salt and light" to the world around us, and we are to be the "fragrance of Christ among those who are being saved and among those who are perishing" (2 Cor. 2:15).

Today we look around at the condition of our school systems, our broken families, the crime and violence taking place daily, and we blame everyone else for what we see. Then in our self-righteousness, we brush off our hands from any sense of responsibility and back as far away from the problems as possible, distancing ourselves from the sin. But if our city is in disorder, it can only be a reflection of the disorder in the church; ultimately the church is responsible for being the agent of change and reformation in our society.

The church tends to protest strongly against "really bad" sin like abortion or homosexuality—sins that are more obvious. The problem is that much of the sin we protest against in the world is just as prevalent in the church! Has our religious zeal blinded us to our own condition so that we point out the plank in someone else's eye?

Jesus directed a scathing message to the Pharisees, saying "Woe to you, teachers of the law and Pharisees, you hypocrites! You shut the kingdom of heaven in men's faces. You yourselves do not enter, nor will you let those enter who are trying to" (Matt. 23:14 NIV). The word *hypocrite* in the Greek meant to be an actor in a play, someone who was not expected to live in his daily life what he portrayed in front of people.

Jesus went on to call the Pharisees "whitewashed tombs," saying that although they look beautiful on the outside, the reality is what is on the inside, which Jesus said included "dead men's bones and everything unclean." Although they appeared to other people as righteous, they were full of "hypocrisy and wickedness" (Matt. 23:27–28 NIV).

## Religious Spirit

The most deadly enemy we face in the church is the religious spirit. In some ways everything else we have talked about fits into this category.

The religious spirit is the counterfeit of life and love. It's a "form of godliness but denies the power" (2 Tim. 3:5). It leaves hearts cold and sick in its wake. It replaces simplicity and power with human wisdom and agendas, fellowship with Jesus with rituals, and forms barriers to souls looking for a real Savior.

When the presence of Jesus is not manifest in the church in a tangible way and we continue in our programs, we are inviting the religious spirit to set up her throne in our congregations and ministries. This spirit is more than happy to become a substitute for Jesus; in fact, it's been the goal of the enemy all along.

Eventually, as the church grows more and more compromised and disconnected from Jesus and from her ministry in the world, two things happen: True believers will leave the empty institutionalized church in pursuit of life and intimacy with Jesus, and others will remain, determined to shape and mold it after their own image.

# Chapter 6

# A DISORIENTED CHURCH

"I KNOW YOUR WORKS, THAT YOU ARE
NEITHER COLD NOR HOT. I COULD WISH YOU
WERE COLD OR HOT. SO THEN, BECAUSE YOU
ARE LUKEWARM, AND NEITHER COLD NOR HOT,
I WILL SPEW YOU OUT OF MY MOUTH. BECAUSE
YOU SAY: I AM RICH, HAVE BECOME WEALTHY,
AND HAVE NEED OF NOTHING—AND DO NOT
KNOW THAT YOU ARE WRETCHED, MISERABLE,
POOR, BLIND, AND NAKED."

REVELATION 3:15–17

There is a direct correlation between God's presence and life in a community. Throughout the Bible we see that when God's people lived in obedience, God's favor, blessings, and presence were among them. On the other hand, when God's people rebelled against Him and turned to idolatry, His presence withdrew and the consequences to the people included loss of life, blessing, and freedom. Nations were conquered or liberated according to whether or not the people of God were living righteously in faithful covenant with Him.

When God's presence ceases to be a tangible reality in a community or nation, spiritual life cannot be sustained for long. The second law of thermodynamics states that energy and matter tend to dissipate, i.e., run down, not up; move from order toward chaos; and degenerate from harmonious complexity to random disorder. The measure of this disorder is called entropy. The Bible reveals that spiritual and moral entropy was introduced to the human race through the sin and fall of Adam. Without the intervention of God's grace and power, the direction of things spiritually and morally is downward, not upward. Everything moves toward decline, decay, and death apart from God's intervention. Revival and community transformation are God's ways of countering this law in its spiritual and moral dimensions.

When God's presence begins to recede from a place, the goodness of God—His light and His life—begins to grow fainter and darkness begins to increase and take hold. A number of things follow. First, the people of God slowly become desensitized to the loss of His presence and to the growing darkness around them. As a result, hearts become hardened, senses are dulled, and perspective is lost. So when warnings are sounded to turn back to God, people are more irritated by the jarring comments than filled with conviction and alarm. Over time the vacuum of the loss of God's manifest presence among His people acts like an anesthetic and numbs people to the warnings that always precede judgment.

We must treasure His presence and be alarmed when He withdraws it! We must identify and repent of those things that have offended God and caused Him to withdraw His presence.

## Taken Captive

One of the recurring ways God dealt with His people in the Old Testament was to allow them to be plundered, removed from the land of promise in humiliation, and led away into exile and captivity by foreign nations. This happened to both the northern kingdom, Israel, who was taken into Assyrian captivity, and to the southern kingdom, Judah, at the hands of the Babylonian Empire.

As a result of the Babylonian invasions of the southern kingdom, the city of Jerusalem was destroyed along with the temple. Jeremiah, a prophet of that time, prophesied to the people for more than forty years, warning them repeatedly of the consequences of their personal and collective sin and God's impending judgment. "'For I have set My face against this city for adversity and not for good,' says the Lord.

'It shall be given into the hand of the king of Babylon, and he shall burn it with fire'" (Jer. 21:10).

During each of the three campaigns against Jerusalem, the people of God were carried away captive to Babylon, a pagan nation. Even in the midst of the destruction and captivity of the people, Jeremiah's prophetic warnings went unheeded.

God states clearly in His message to the captives through the prophet Jeremiah that His instruction is "to all those *I carried* into exile from Jerusalem to Babylon." Notice God didn't say "whom Nebuchadnezzar carried into captivity," but rather whom "I carried into captivity." They weren't *taken* captive—God *carried* them into captivity! He was directly responsible for their situation.

Imagine your city or nation being invaded by a foreign army and ten thousand of its citizens being taken captive—carried away to live and serve another government for seventy years! Imagine your city being totally destroyed by an enemy, everything laid waste. But what if God had been warning you for forty years? It's hard to imagine that humans can be so stubborn and rebellious that they actually ignore God's warnings of impending destruction, but that's exactly what the people of God did. That's why we need to leave our captivity when God is still giving us opportunity to do so.

When God's people drift away from Him, they become easy targets of the enemy and succumb to idolatry and sin. As a result, God begins to withdraw His presence from among His people and captivity results. We as the church then become "exiled" from our identity and purpose.

In his challenging book *Prophetic Untimeliness* Oz Guiness makes the observation: "The crying need of the western church today is for reformation and revival and for a decisive liberation from the Babylonian captivity of modernity."[1] The longer God's people remain in captivity, the less willing they are to struggle with the challenges of the modern world. In our pursuit of relevance, we have simply adopted the culture of the world around us. While we must be relevant in communicating the message of the gospel, it can't be according to fads or trends picked up from this present world.

## Church in Captivity

What about us? Where are we in the Western world? Are we in a state of captivity? How do we know? When you look at how the corporate church is functioning in society, there are several things that help us evaluate whether we are functioning in freedom, and therefore effectiveness, or captivity and resulting ineffectiveness.

For example, the term *Christian* means different things to different people. To some, it's almost synonymous with being a "good" American or being a member of a church, even if the church is nominal or lukewarm. To others it refers to a general inclination or religious preference for Christianity over other religions, such as Buddhism or Hinduism. For still others it refers to very specific values, beliefs, and lifestyle parameters.

Trying to understand these various expressions of "faith" is complicated. How do you describe faith? It's like trying to describe beauty, happiness, or contentment. Faith is a complex grouping of ideas, emotions, experiences, and truth that is difficult to quantify or explain. Therefore, it is helpful to rely upon measurements of how faith is integrated into people's lives, what kind of influence it has on their situation and life practices.

The Barna Research Group has been the leader in researching trends in the American church for over twenty years. They have carefully analyzed the Christian population according to their faith commitment. To do this, Barna works with three categories of "Christians":

(1) *evangelicals*—those who believe their relationship with Jesus Christ will provide them with eternal life and who accept the Bible as being accurate and authoritative.

(2) *non-evangelical born again Christians* who believe they have eternal salvation through the grace given them by God through their faith in Christ but do not believe in various core doctrines taught in the Bible.

(3) *notional Christians*—those who consider themselves as Christians in their "religious orientation" and usually believe they will go to heaven for some reason other than Christ's death and resurrection. Others confess they do not know their eternal destiny. This category of Christians generally does not embrace core biblical doctrines.[2]

## How Saved Are We?

Let's take a look at the reported evidence on the condition of the American church:

While 85 percent of Americans call themselves "Christians," only 41 percent of them have been born again. Of the 41 percent of Americans that have been born again, only 7 percent are "evangelical" in their theology, meaning they accept the Bible as accurate and authoritative.

By definition, this evangelical group would agree that their faith is important in their life today, that they have a responsibility to share their faith, that Satan is real, that eternal salvation is by grace not works, that Jesus lived a sinless life on earth, and that God is an all-knowing, all-powerful deity who created the universe and still rules it today.[3]

Other interesting facts include the following:

- Fifty percent of adults who say they are Christians are not "absolutely committed" to the Christian faith.[4]
- Nearly 50 percent of all non-evangelical born again Christians believe that Jesus did not lead a sinless life.[5]
- Sixty-two percent of born again Christians do not believe that Satan is real but believe he is merely a symbol of evil.[6]
- Forty-one percent of adults who attend Christian church services in a typical week are not born again believers.[7]

It is clearly evident from Barna's research statistics that the church has become biblically, theologically, and morally confused. The Scripture tells us that a double-minded man is unstable in all his ways (James 1:8). This instability has had a very serious impact on our communities.

The gap between what we call ourselves and what we are committed to live out in reality is wide. We call ourselves Christian, but we aren't living according to biblical Christianity.

For example, how can people share their faith with an unbeliever if they aren't convinced Jesus led a sinless life? Is He a savior or does He also need a savior? And how can we evangelize our community if the majority of the Christians don't believe hell or Satan are real? If Jesus isn't the perfect Son of God who purchased humanity with His blood to save them from eternal destruction, then what's the point? In that scenario, there isn't one. And that's exactly where our society is directing us—to reject absolute truth.

The church's role as salt and light in society is diminishing at an alarming pace. The foundation of kingdom values both in the church and in the world is being rejected. The faith of millions of people no longer rests on kingdom values, such as holiness, integrity, respect, acceptance of absolutes, and reverence for God. "The rejection of these elements has created a void that has been filled by the customized spirituality that lacks biblical moorings."[8]

In December 2003 the Barna Research Group summarized the spiritual climate of the nation in a report with the following excerpts:

### Millions of Americans Are Spiritually Satisfied—and Confused

Contradictions and confusion permeate the spiritual condition of the nation. Studies conducted during 2003 indicate, for instance, that while 84 percent of adults say their religious faith is very important in their own life, 66 percent also say that religion is losing influence in the nation. While people are clearly spending less time involved in religious practices such as Bible reading, prayer, and participating in church activities, 70 percent claim that their own religious faith is consistently growing deeper.

This year brought about increases in the proportions of people who contend that cohabitation (60%), adultery (42%), sexual relations between homosexuals (30%), abortion (45%), pornography (38%), the use of profanity (36%), and gambling (61%) are "morally acceptable" behaviors.

Even perceptions regarding eternal salvation reflect confusion. Although just 38 percent of the adult public have confessed their sins and accepted Christ as their savior, 99 percent claim they will not go to hell after they die. In fact, a majority of Americans do not believe that Satan exists and most adults are uncertain about the existence of hell.

America's spiritual confusion undoubtedly relates to the fact that most people own a Bible but few know what's in it. Research showing that only 4 percent of all adults and just 9 percent of born again Christians have a biblical worldview sheds light on the distorted viewpoints that reign in the United States.

### Lots of Religious Activity But Limited Gains Are Evident

What makes all of these realities so hard to grasp is the substantial level of religious activity in the United States. Christian ministries will raise nearly $60 billion for domestic ministry in 2003, and there is an estimated $3 billion of new construction work occurring on church properties to facilitate expanded ministry activities. All of these figures lend an air of security and stability to the religious condition of the country.

However, it is that very degree of continuity, when connected with the moral decay, family and parenting struggles, financial challenges, and educational demise, that gives reason to question the spiritual health of the nation. The fact that there has not been any measurable increase in church involvement or personal spiritual depth in the past decade challenges the widespread notion that the United States is as spiritually healthy and focused as ever.[9]

- Our double-mindedness has made us unstable and confused.
- Our idolatry has offended God and caused Him to withdraw His presence and glory.
- He is opposed to our pride and rejects our self-righteousness.
- Our lack of holiness has given our enemy the opportunity to plunder us.
- Our alliances with the world system have robbed us of our spiritual authority and have left us powerless.
- Our deception has led us into complacency, captivity, and hopelessness.

As spiritual compromise continues to seep into our culture like a polluted river, the enemy has a weapon of choice that protects his agenda—the demand for tolerance. The highest value in our culture right now is personal rights, personal freedom, and personal morality/spirituality. No matter what evil practice or rebellious attitude surfaces, it is quickly embraced and protected in the name of "tolerance." It seems that the only people who don't benefit from this consideration are Bible-believing Christians!

This is an ever-evident battle between the kingdom of God and the kingdom of the world. The kingdoms are in conflict; they are not and will never be in harmony! Jesus said that people who love darkness hate the light and avoid coming into the light for fear that their deeds will be exposed (John 3:20).

When the darkness in the world begins to infiltrate the church and compromise begins to overtake righteousness, relativism and humanism become confused with real Christian faith. When our faith has successfully been redefined by the spirit of the world, we have lost the battle.

General William Booth, the founder of The Salvation Army, made a profoundly accurate prediction when he said, "I consider that the chief dangers which will confront the twentieth century will be: religion without the Holy Spirit, Christianity without Christ, forgiveness without regeneration, morality without God, heaven without hell."[10]

## IMPACT OF OUR CAPTIVITY IN THE CITY

We are in a state of spiritual captivity! Since the church is intended to be God's dwelling place in a city or community, if His presence is no longer tangible in the church, it can no longer be manifested in the city either. We don't have to look very hard to see the social and moral devastation around us. God doesn't leave quickly; He doesn't get offended and stomp off in a righteous huff. God pleads with His people to turn aside from idolatry and come back to intimacy with Him. God withdraws His glory both reluctantly and gradually. He lingers as long as He can, waiting for any indication from His people to cause Him to relent.

In every testimony of a transformed community and in revival history, God's people became aware of their captivity and then made a conscious decision to break agreements with strongholds of the enemy. In communities gripped by addictions, crime, and abuse, the church has taken a stand and said no to the enemy and cried out to God for deliverance. As they walked out the Lord's instruction in 2 Chronicles 7:14 and "turned from their wicked ways," God heard their prayer and healed their communities.

## GOD'S MOTIVATION

The primary motivation of God's heart in dealing with such serious issues in His church is jealousy for His bride. God is always motivated by love, and sometimes His love is fierce.

"For the Lord your God is a consuming fire, a jealous God" (Deut. 4:24). "You shall worship no other god, for the Lord, whose name is Jealous, is a jealous God" (Ex. 34:14).

In his book *Enjoying God* S. J. Hill makes a powerful comment on the jealousy of God, saying that "at the core of God's personality is an all-consuming fire of love called jealousy. His jealousy is not the by-product of insecurity or mistrust, nor is it destructive. Holy jealousy is an intense passion to protect a love relationship that's priceless and to avenge it when it's fractured. God's holy anger at any threat to this relationship is in direct proportion to the burning fire of His love. He will not tolerate any rivals in His relationship with His people."[11]

Jesus died to deliver us from captivity and to give us abundant life. He didn't pay such a high price for our redemption so we could live mediocre lives, ensnared in the world system and clueless about our identity and purpose! God's motivation in exposing our compromise is so that we can be delivered from it and live life filled with His highest purpose.

God is shifting our paradigms, challenging our methodologies, and inviting us to one of the greatest challenges the church has ever faced: a return to her first love. God is challenging His church to leave her lukewarm Western-church culture and return to covenant relationship with Him and live according to the truth of His Word.

## Chapter 7

# EVIDENCE OF CAPTIVITY

"GO, AND TELL THIS PEOPLE: 'KEEP ON HEARING,
BUT DO NOT UNDERSTAND; KEEP ON SEEING,
BUT DO NOT PERCEIVE.' MAKE THE HEART OF
THIS PEOPLE DULL, AND THEIR EARS HEAVY, AND
SHUT THEIR EYES; LEST THEY SEE WITH THEIR
EYES, AND HEAR WITH THEIR EARS, AND
UNDERSTAND WITH THEIR HEART, AND RETURN
AND BE HEALED."

ISAIAH 6:9–10

When we look at the condition of our communities, we cannot blame our political or social institutions. We can't even blame the devil! The only institution responsible for regulating the spiritual climate of a community is the church of the Lord Jesus Christ. A strong, vibrant church can survive the greatest oppression. Consider the underground church in China! More than thirty thousand people are being saved there *every day*! In the midst of great persecution, the church prevails. Yet in the Western church, we are struggling to influence our culture—not because of persecution or great oppression, but because of other strongholds. Our greatest enemies in the Western world are materialism, spiritual pride, complacency, and self-sufficiency.

As the church has increasingly compromised and succumbed to

the cultural values and lifestyle of the world, her spiritual senses and mission have become dulled. What causes captivity? Things such as idolatry, compromise, disobedience, pride, greed, deception, slumber, or agreement with the enemy. We become vulnerable to captivity when we aren't praying, aren't spending time with the Lord, or become isolated from healthy relationships.

Scripture promises us in Matthew 16:18 that God will build His church and the gates of hell "shall not prevail against it." What are the things trying to prevail against the church? Have they gained a foothold? Let's look at a couple of indicators of captivity in our Western church:

## COUNTERCULTURE VERSUS SUBCULTURE

To what extent has the Western culture, values, and worldview infiltrated the church? What are some of those values and how do they compare to biblical values? Some Western world values include: independence and individuality, materialistic success, sexual freedom and sensual pleasure, self-seeking, self-protection, and the need to be in control. We place high value on the mind, the intellect, education, knowledge, strength, and ambition. We value being a self-made people. The pioneer spirit has so permeated American culture that we strive to make our own way, to conquer and prevail. Do you ever see these values evident in the church?

When Jesus came to the earth, He introduced a culture that was radical and totally foreign to the culture of His day. He turned the political and social systems upside down by introducing the culture of the kingdom of God.

Jesus introduced this new culture—or new covenant—in His Sermon on the Mount teaching (Matthew 5–7). Jesus boldly proclaimed a *new* value system, including such radical concepts as loving your enemies, praying in secret, and storing up treasures in heaven. He said that those who mourn, those who hunger and thirst, those who are poor in spirit, and those who are merciful will be blessed. Following His introduction of this new value system of the kingdom of God, He talked about being the salt and light in society.

When Jesus began to teach people about the kingdom of God, the Bible says that the "people were astonished at His teaching, for He taught them as one having authority" (Matt. 7:28–29). This did not happen in the temple when the Sadducees taught the law or in the synagogues when the rabbis taught the Scriptures. Jesus stepped into His society as an agent of change, as a transformer, a life-changer. He introduced a kingdom not of this world. The kingdom of God that Jesus proclaimed was a counterculture that confronted the culture of His day. The hungry and desperate were drawn to this good news; the religious leaders rejected it.

The truth is, we in the Western church have become a *subculture* instead of a *counterculture*. A subculture can only reflect the value system and worldview of the culture of which it is a part. Therefore, a subculture cannot be an agent of change because by definition it has become part of the culture it is trying to affect.

The church is not meant to be a maintenance organization. We are supposed to be change agents in our communities! When we are double-minded and unstable, we cannot influence our culture.

What about the culture of the Western church? What are we reflecting—the culture of the world or the culture of the kingdom of God? The church has lost its way and desperately needs a spiritual and moral revival to become a counterculture. We have lost sight of the values of the kingdom of God, such as contentment, being God-centered not self-centered, serving rather than receiving, being of no reputation, being dependent and weak. Values of God's kingdom, such as sacrificing, suffering, walking by faith and not by sight, and giving what we have away have been forgotten in our quest for worldly status. Everything we do should be for eternal benefit, not shortsighted, temporal gains in this world.

During Jesus' time of testing in the wilderness, it was Satan who tempted Him. He was offered the kingdoms of the world with all their glory, but He refused. Jesus knew there was a real kingdom and a real glory, and He was not about to settle for a counterfeit. Neither should we!

The kingdom Jesus brought to us is not of this world. The question for us, then, is: Where are we living—in the reality of God's kingdom or in the world? Are you living as an agent of change or following the status quo? God is looking for revolutionaries! It's time to stop trying to "add" Jesus into *our* culture and step into *His* kingdom!

## LACK OF SPIRITUAL AUTHORITY

When we are not essentially any different from the non-Christian culture we live in, we don't have spiritual authority. God desires that His church walk in much more spiritual authority and power than we have seen so far!

Do you ever get tired of praying for people without seeing results? We are trying to influence and impact so many things, but we simply don't have spiritual authority because of the compromise and idolatry in the house of God. We have been trying to convince God to act in power while ignoring clear principles in His Word. He is stopping us in our tracks!

People in our cities have desperate needs. What would happen in a city if a desperate parent brought a child to the church for deliverance and healing, like the man who brought his child to Jesus in Matthew 17?

> "Lord, have mercy on my son, for he is an epileptic and suffers severely; for he often falls into the fire and often into the water. And I brought him to Your disciples, and they could not cure him." Then Jesus answered and said, "O faithless and perverse generation, how long shall I be with you? How long shall I bear with you? Bring him here to Me." And Jesus rebuked him, and the demon came out of him; and the child was cured from that very hour. Then the disciples came to Jesus privately and said, "Why could we not cast him out?" And Jesus said to them, "Because of your unbelief; however, this kind does not go out except by prayer and fasting" (Matthew 17:15–21).

Jesus pointed to their failure and called them "unbelieving." While the Lord regularly challenged His disciples in the Gospels for their hardness of heart, dullness, and unbelief, in Acts we see these same disciples ministering with great authority and effectiveness. Fortunately, they didn't stay in this place of unbelief!

## SELF-VALIDATION

It's almost funny sometimes how indignant Christians can be when it's suggested that the church is compromised or has wandered away from her first love. The world around us is aware of our compromised, ineffective condition, but we continue in our same routines as though everything is going well.

We have become convinced of our own methods and ability to remain effective in ministry whether or not Jesus is involved in the process. The church has become a well-trained institution, and the reality is that we are capable of functioning with or without the manifest presence of God. That is alarming.

Although the majority of church leaders in the United States report they are content with the effectiveness of their ministries and feel they are doing an excellent or at least a good job, the facts of research suggest something very different. George Barna summarizes recent findings:

> It is a bit troubling to see pastors feel they're doing a great job when the research reveals that few congregants have a biblical worldview, half the people they minister to are not spiritually secure or developed, kids are fleeing from the church in record numbers, most of the people who attend worship services admit they did not connect with God, the divorce rate among Christians is no different than that of non-Christians, only 2% of the pastors themselves can identify God's vision for their ministry they are trying to lead, and the average congregant spends more time watching television in one day than he spends in all spiritual pursuits combined for an entire week. It's worrisome when there is a strong correlation between church size and self-satisfaction, because that suggests that attendance and budget figures have become our mark of success. It's troubling when our spiritual leaders cannot articulate where we are headed and how the church will fulfill its role as the restorative agent of our society. Maybe the comfort afforded by our buildings and other material possessions has seduced us into thinking we are farther down the road than we really are.[1]

THE GAP BETWEEN OUR PERCEPTION OF OUR EFFECTIVENESS AND THE REALITY OF OUR EFFECTIVENESS STEMS FROM OUR CONTINUED SELF-VALIDATION.

Regardless of its true purpose and intent, the Christian community is not known for love or for its transforming faith. As a result, the United States remains one of the largest mission fields in the world. Of course that is *not* how we perceive ourselves. For the most part, American Christians see themselves as the most highly developed Christian nation, the ones who spread the gospel to the rest of the needy world. But the reality is that we have become a mission field ourselves!

Do you want an eye-opening assignment? Ask somebody outside your local congregation how effective your ministry is in the city or community where you live. Ask a neighbor, friend, or a complete stranger what their perception is of the effectiveness of the Christian church in your city. I asked that question of a hotel manager in a city I was visiting. I asked him, "How effective would you say the Christian church has been in affecting your life in the city? Has your life been impacted at all, have any of your needs been met through the church? Have you been ministered to or encouraged in any way?" It's an interesting topic, because most people don't even realize that the church is *supposed* to be ministering to them. It's good for us to start asking practical questions outside the walls of our congregations and then determining our ministry course of action and evaluation based on the answers we get.

The gap between our perception of our effectiveness and the reality of our effectiveness stems from our continued self-validation. Rather than measuring ourselves by biblical standards for effective ministry—the lost being saved and becoming disciples, the number of believers in a city increasing, believers developing character and effectiveness—we instead compare ourselves with one another. Then, depending on whether we compare ourselves to another ministry that is doing better or worse than we are, we either rest in prideful self-satisfaction or become ambitious and competitive out of our insecurity.

There are real dangers and pitfalls when the church becomes disconnected with the world around us and measures herself against herself rather than measuring her true effectiveness in the larger community. The world observes and determines our relevance and effectiveness and then makes decisions about trusting us and believing our message, ultimately deciding if they believe Jesus is who He says He is. John 17:23 says that the world will know who He is by the unity found in His church. The world questions our relevance and doesn't believe we have any real spiritual power. They probably figure if we had authority and power, we would use it.

## DIMINISHED FEAR OF THE LORD

If the presence of the living God is glorious and powerful, it is also fearful. His manifest presence brings people from every walk of life to a place where they fear the name of the Lord. The reason the world doesn't fear Him is because the church doesn't fear Him! For many years the church has been missing a visitation of the fear of

> THE REASON THE WORLD DOESN'T FEAR HIM IS BECAUSE THE CHURCH DOESN'T FEAR HIM!

God. How can we fear Him whose power we have never experienced? We talk about it, but never really understand it. Being struck by a lightning bolt would leave a permanent memory, as does a genuine encounter with God![2]

Our sanctuaries and worship services are designed to make us feel comfortable. We want a place where we can meet God on our terms. It's a curious thing how we think about God's presence and then try to fit it into our lives in an acceptable and predictable way. The church sanctuary may be full on a Sunday morning, but what drew the people? Is it the supernatural presence of God, the charismatic personality of the senior pastor, or the new youth program?

There is nothing wrong with having a comfortable worship environment or good ministry programs, but the question is, Are we gathering people to meet with and enjoy one another's company or to encounter the Lord and be changed by His?

"A holy fear or reverential awe of God can only be realized through an encounter with God as an otherworldly, transcendent, holy, and supernatural reality. Casual, seeker-friendly, routinized 'churchianity' may feel pleasant but it fails to provide the kind of spine-tingling, edge-of-the-seat unpredictability that delivers us from lesser distractions and the pattern of the pagan world culture around us."[3]

I remember the first time I encountered the glory of God. His manifest presence filled the room, and I was terrified! Although I had had encounters with His presence before, this was different. This was

His power—intense and terrifying—during a conference in Argentina. Leaders were beginning to pray for several hundred people in the room. The presence and weight of God's glory began to overwhelm us. I'll never forget the way my heart started to pound as the presence of God drew nearer to me. I remember thinking, *If He gets any closer, it will kill me.*

His presence was almost suffocating in its power and strength. I had mixed feelings—should I run away from it or toward it? The wind of God's Spirit moved through the room that night, and He left a trail like a tornado had swept through the place. People were on their faces crying out to God. Some had been thrown several feet by His power and were lying under tables and against the back wall. Many were experiencing spontaneous deliverance as the Holy Spirit washed over them; still others were laughing with joy after receiving deep emotional healing.

I'm not quite sure what all happened, but one thing was evident: God had visited us in a fullness that I had never encountered before. His presence was uncontrollable, unpredictable, and powerful in His ability to heal and deliver. His manifest presence was unmistakable, and my encounter with Him changed me forever.

THERE IS NO EXPECTATION OF HIS PRESENCE IN OUR SANCTUARIES!

Isaiah's encounter with the presence of God was especially dramatic. The posts of the door were shaken by the voice of the angel announcing God's holiness and glory. The house was filled with smoke (the Shekinah glory). Isaiah responded by crying out, "Woe is me, for I am undone! Because I am a man of unclean lips, and I dwell in the midst of a people of unclean lips." How did Isaiah know his lips and those of his people were unclean? "For my eyes have seen the King, the Lord of hosts" (Isa. 6:5).

John Mulinde, a pastor and spiritual leader in Uganda who is featured on the second *Transformations* video,[4] shares an interesting thing that is happening in his congregation. Now that the manifest presence of God is present in their sanctuary, people stop on the threshold of the door into the sanctuary in a holy fear of God, because they know the presence of the living God is dwelling on the other side!

His Shekinah glory is present, and it has caused a reverential fear and trembling in the people who attend the services.

How do we enter the sanctuaries of our congregations? Do we pause in awe of the Lord, expecting Him to be present on the other side of the door? Or do we just walk in chatting with one another, find our seats, and wait for the service to begin? There is no expectation of His presence in our sanctuaries!

Without the manifest presence of the Lord, there is no fear of God. We need to encounter Him before we can fear Him.

## CHRONIC SPIRITUAL BOREDOM

The Western world church is being saturated with an ever-increasing Laodicean culture. We have been lulled to sleep! This has resulted in an epidemic of bored, dissatisfied believers. Being a passionate follower of Christ isn't easy or popular; it's much more respectable in our culture to be people who just go with the flow. But where is the "flow" going?

The answer to this problem isn't programmatic; we must revive our spiritual passion! It takes much more energy to contend for spiritual passion and to insist that we must have God's presence. But making our pursuit of the presence of Jesus our highest priority ensures that our lives will be filled with fascination, adventure, and mystery. Without Him, we become entangled in the world, which cannot satisfy our deepest longings.

The more time between regular tangible encounters with Jesus, the more bored we become. The sobering reality is that after a while we actually lose our appetite for God and spiritual "atrophy" occurs; we lose our spiritual muscle and become weak and flabby. Reducing our faith to the lowest common denominator cannot satisfy the deep longings of our hearts and doesn't leave much to offer others either.

Jesus admonishes the church of Ephesus, saying, "I have this against you, that you have left your first love" (Rev. 2:4). This is the wake-up call of Jesus! Like the church of Ephesus, many believers today have lost their first love, turning instead to routines and methods that result in complacency and dullness that are grievous to God. Paul exhorts believers, "Wake up, O sleeper, rise from the dead" (Eph. 5:14 NIV).

The human heart was created to be fascinated, not bored. We

were created to love and live in fellowship with our amazing, glorious God and to participate with Him in divine purposes. There is no good reason for a believer in Jesus Christ to be bored. We have the opportunity to participate in the greatest adventure imaginable!

We must contend earnestly for our faith. We must fight through the complacency and lethargy of the flesh, a compromised church, and the devil's persistence in discouraging us. Only by contending will we find spiritual victory. How much more of God do we want? Do we want a *little* more anointing in our worship services, or do we want enough to turn our city and nation upside down with a holy revolution?

## DELIVERERS

The good news is that when God's people are in captivity, He desires that we be free and so prepares us for deliverance. He raised up deliverers like Joseph, Moses, John the Baptist, and ultimately Jesus, to bring His people out of bondage.

One of the purposes of the book of Daniel is to reassure God's covenant people that their judgment of captivity is not permanent. The Lord in His mercy continued to speak to them through the prophets, giving the people a sense of expectancy for freedom and restoration. Ezekiel prophesied for God during his captivity in Babylon:

> "I will give you a new heart and put a new spirit within you, I will take the heart of stone out of your flesh and give you a heart of flesh. I will put My Spirit within you and cause you to walk in My statutes, and you will keep My judgments and do them. Then you shall dwell in the land that I gave to your fathers; you shall be My people, and I will be your God" (Ezekiel 36:26–28).

Daniel read Jeremiah 29, believed its prophetic promise, and began to declare it as a young man in Babylon. God prepared Daniel and other prophets who prophesied during captivity, and the people held on to the promises of God given through them and waited for their day of deliverance.

Today the stage is set for a mighty breakthrough! The church is poised for revival because God always sends it when we need it.

When the time for deliverance comes, the Lord begins to set things in motion—He raises up deliverers, prophetic voices that cry out for deliverance. If we cry out, God will deliver us. He promises:

> "I will bring health and healing to it; I will heal my people and will let them enjoy abundant peace and security. I will bring Judah and Israel back from captivity and will rebuild them as they were before. I will cleanse them from all the sin they have committed against me and will forgive all their sins of rebellion against me" (Jeremiah 33:6–8 NIV).

What an amazing promise! Not only does God promise them deliverance from their captivity but also restoration of their city, forgiveness for their sins, healing, and abundant peace! God is a holistic God. He doesn't only respond to what we think we need—He wants to bring healing and restoration to who we are and to the cities and communities we live in.

Throughout church history God has raised up men and women who have been instruments in His hand to stir His people for revival. They were usually obscure, unknown, and sometimes a bit unusual. Take for example the young coal miner Evan Roberts, whom God used to bring the Welsh Revival. Roberts wasn't an eloquent preacher or gifted with a great intellect, but He possessed a burning passion for Jesus. Roberts cried out for revival day and night in prayer without ceasing for thirteen years before the Welsh Revival began.

Throughout the revival Evan Roberts constantly stressed the necessity of dealing honestly with sin, complete obedience to the Holy Spirit, and the preeminence of the Lord Jesus Christ. Roberts was instrumental in bringing healing to an entire country because he cared, he wept, and he prayed. He embraced the broken heart of God and offered it back up through prayer and intercession. As a result, "wherever he went, hearts were set aflame with the love of God!"[5]

## CRYING OUT IN THE MIDST OF CAPTIVITY!

During the ominous days of war and imminent captivity for Judah, God sent His prophets to both warn and encourage the people about His promises. We often quote Jeremiah 29:11: "'For I know the thoughts that I think toward you,' says the Lord, 'thoughts of peace and not of evil, to give you a future and a hope.'" We apply it to ourselves and our friends to encourage us about God's good plans for our lives. It's important to note, however, the historical context of this verse. God wasn't only encouraging the Jewish people about their future; Jeremiah was writing to some who were hostages, living in the midst of captivity in Babylon.

The message God gave through Jeremiah was unique in its instruction to the people in captivity. God didn't tell them to *hang on; this will soon be over; stick together.* He said,

> "Build houses and settle down; plant gardens and eat what they produce. Marry and have sons and daughters; find wives for your sons and give your daughters in marriage, so that they too may have sons and daughters. Increase in number there; do not decrease. Also, seek the peace and prosperity of the city to which I have carried you into exile. Pray to the Lord for it, because if it prospers, you too will prosper" (Jeremiah 29:5–7 NIV).

God encouraged the people to settle in the city and bless it while they were there, saying they would prosper as a result. Not only was God working on the hearts of rebellious Israel, He also had a plan for the pagan nation of Babylon. Look what He says in verse 10: "When seventy years are completed for Babylon, I will come to you and fulfill my gracious promise to bring you back to this place." God didn't say "when seventy years are completed for Judah" but *for Babylon!* God's timetable for releasing the captives had as much to do with what He was working into the nation of Babylon as it did for Judah.

God not only used Babylon as a punishment for His rebellious people, He also used His desperate and broken people in captivity as an instrument of grace deposited within the nation of Babylon. Remember King Nebuchadnezzar? Remember Daniel? They are part of an amazing story that unfolded in the nation of Babylon during the captivity of Judah. Daniel was a young man when he was taken captive. He was a contemporary of Jeremiah and served as a prophet during the period of captivity. Daniel and his friends had a tremendous impact on the nation as a result of their fervent intercession and faithfulness to the Lord. They influenced Babylonian government, kings, and the people who lived there.

Daniel remained separate from the pagan culture, devout, careful not to compromise his conscience by eating rich foods. He impacted the surrounding culture by the intimacy he had with God, by his sincere devotion, his prayer life, and the gifts God gave him. God set up situations where Daniel could impact even the king of Babylon, and therefore the kingdom/nation. The ends of chapters 3 and 4 in Daniel make startling confessions about God—check them out!

The devotion of Shadrach, Meshach, and Abed-Nego and God's deliverance of them from the fire caused wicked King Nebuchadnezzar to praise God, saying, "There is no other God who can deliver like this" (Dan. 3:29b).

When there is a functioning priesthood in a city, even a pagan city can be affected by one godly man—like Daniel—who is present.

## HOW DO WE RESPOND?

The church today is like the woman caught in adultery. We are guilty as charged! But we must respond like Jesus did, not the religious leaders. They wanted Jesus to apply the law so that they could stone the woman, but the real motive was to test Jesus—what would He do with her? Jesus challenged the religious leaders by inviting those without sin to cast the first stone. Then He spoke to the woman after He had dealt with her accusers and instructed her to "go and sin no more" (John 8:11).

We must respond to the condition of the church like Nehemiah did when he heard of the condition of Jerusalem—by praying, weeping, and repenting. When God's glory is not manifest in the church, we must demonstrate 2 Chronicles 7:14, by coming before God with humility, prayer, and repentance, by seeking His face and turning from our "wicked ways." We must decide to stop being content with His absence and refuse to continue to live in our current spiritual condition!

The exiles of Israel and Judah into captivity actually led to the recovery of their identity and purpose as a nation. The trauma and oppression of captivity caused them to cry out in desperation to God, and actually served to restore God's remnant back to faithfulness and obedience.

We are in a dangerous place spiritually when we come to regard the lack of God's presence and the resulting captivity of the church as "normal." Jesus told the church at Laodicea that it is better to be hot or cold than to be lukewarm (see Revelation 3:14–20). In a spiritually lukewarm environment, religion becomes mere doctrine, an intellectual pursuit. When the hearts of believers are no longer engaged in their experience of God, He becomes a separate category from the rest of life. The church becomes less and less separate from the world and is affected more and more by the universities, the media, and cultural values that preach a relativistic morality.

Our response to the condition of the church must be to wait on the Lord until He revives and restores us, not to search for a program to try to bolster our condition with false hope.

> "You will seek Me and find Me, when you search for Me with all your heart. I will be found by you, says the Lord, and I will bring you back from your captivity; I will gather you from all the nations and from all the places where I have driven you, says the Lord, and I will bring you to the place from which I cause you to be carried away captive" (Jeremiah 29:13–14).

We must cry out in desperation to be released from our captivity! Psalm 106 says that even though the people of Israel rebelled, God "regarded their affliction, when he heard their cry; And he remembered for them his covenant, and repented according to the multitude of his mercies" (106:44–45 KJV). When we acknowledge our true condition and cry out for deliverance, God will not only deliver us but will also restore us to obedience and faithfulness, resulting in His manifest presence among us. Who will lead the church out of captivity? Where are the leaders like Moses, Gideon, or Daniel? Where are the John the Baptists of our generation?

Beloved, Jesus wants His church back—He is moving toward us with urgency and zeal to capture the hearts of His people again. He is drawing us out of captivity and inviting us into destiny. *There is hope!*

## Chapter 8

# INVITATION TO THE WILDERNESS

"BEHOLD, I WILL ALLURE HER, [I] WILL BRING
HER INTO THE WILDERNESS, AND SPEAK
COMFORT TO HER."

HOSEA 2:14

Once we have taken an honest look at our condition, what should be our response? Do we work harder? Proceed in denial? Hope that somehow it will all get better? The Lord has an answer for His wandering bride, and He shows us His heart for her in the book of Hosea—it's a trip to the wilderness!

In Hosea, the wilderness is a place of quietness, solitude, and rest. It's a place where the Bridegroom allures His bride to speak tenderly to her and is thus a place of merciful ministry. The story of Hosea is about the relationship between Hosea and his wife, Gomer, who continued to wander from her marriage into adulterous relationships.

This is also a story depicting the relationship between God and His people. This book was written to the northern kingdom of Israel. It's a picture of a disgraceful, idolatrous people chasing after other gods. It's a powerful example of God's love remaining faithful in spite of the unfaithfulness of His people.

"I will punish her for the days she burned incense to the Baals;
she decked herself with rings and jewelry, and went after her lovers,

but me she forgot," declares the Lord. "Therefore I am now going to allure her; I will lead her into the desert and speak tenderly to her" (Hosea 2:13–14 NIV).

In the passage above we can clearly see both God's pain for His wandering bride as well as the invitation He extends to her to repent and return to Him. Jesus doesn't answer all of our questions during a season in the wilderness; rather, He offers himself to us. Jesus draws us out to a quiet place, away from all of our preoccupations, in order to speak tenderly to us and bring healing and restoration. The beauty of God is what "allures" us into the wilderness with Him. It's His love for us that allows us to trust Him even in the seasons of wilderness.

God's heart toward His people has always been the same. He longs for covenant fellowship, and when that fellowship is violated and broken, He extends not only warnings of the consequences but also an invitation filled with mercy to return to Him. How amazing! The love and mercy God extends to us is unfathomable. His love reaches to the highest skies and the deepest seas!

When God first spoke to Jeremiah, He told him to go tell the city of Jerusalem this: "I remember you, the kindness of your youth, the love of your betrothal, when you went after Me in the wilderness" (Jer. 2:2). When God delivered His people from the captivity of Egypt, He led them through the wilderness.

## PREPARATION IN THE WILDERNESS

The wilderness represents several different things in the Bible. It illustrates a place to which God takes His people—a difficult, survival place of solitude, loneliness, and testing. There He works in our lives to bring about redemptive brokenness and to prepare us for usefulness. The experience prepares us to go deeper into our relationship with Jesus so we can possess His promises and realize our destiny.

God likes the wilderness. He uses the wilderness both literally and metaphorically as the place to prepare His people. For Moses, it was an issue of humility. The wilderness became God's means to break his Egyptian arrogance and fleshly confidence in his own ability. After forty years in the wilderness, when God was prepared to use him to deliver Israel from Egypt, Moses no longer felt he could do it and told God to find somebody else! For the nation of Israel, the wilderness season served as a cleansing agent to remove the influence of their many years in Egypt.

God speaks about the wilderness experience for Israel in Deuteronomy 8:2: "The Lord your God led you all the way these forty years in the wilderness, to humble you and test you, to know what was in your heart, whether you would keep His commandments or not." In the wilderness the Lord fed them, provided garments that did not wear out, and trained them, saying, "As a man chastens his son, so the Lord your God chastens you" (Deut. 8:5).

Then God reminds them of His covenant: "For the Lord your God is bringing you into a good land" (Deut. 8:7). God is longing to bring us through the wilderness into the land of promise! For the Israelites, as well as for us, this requires a time of testing and humbling us to "know what is in our hearts."

It was in the wilderness that God prepared and released the forerunner ministry and message of John the Baptist. And it was also in the wilderness where Jesus encountered and resisted Satan as the final step of preparation for His ministry.

## LIFE-CHANGING OPPORTUNITY

Being drawn away by the Lord into a "wilderness" season can be a life-changing opportunity. The season may be long or short, mildly or extremely painful emotionally. We don't go there because we are "bad" or because God is mad at us; He leads us there to perfect His character and nature in us.

When we wander away from our intimacy with the Lord, it seems difficult to follow Him into the wilderness. Once we have wandered away, we are afraid to look into His eyes, fearing we will find anger or, worse, disappointment. So instead of running toward Him, we preoccupy ourselves with lesser things that cannot satisfy us. But if we follow the Lord into this quiet place of intimacy, away from all our preoccupations and wandering, He will gently remove all the traces of Egypt from our lives.

I met a couple recently who had endured a difficult season in the wilderness. As I listened to their story I was moved to tears. Not because of the tremendous pain they had endured, but because of the sweetness of their spirits. They had lost everything, betrayed by a brother they trusted. And although they could have easily fought back and prevailed, they chose not to. Now they were in my office sharing their story—not the pain but the hope. That painful experience became a door for them to enter into a season of wilderness.

I prayed for my new friends at the end of our meeting, and as soon as I placed my hands on their backs, I began to cry. The Lord broke my heart by allowing me to sense a bit of how He felt about them. I wasn't crying because of what they had endured; I was crying at the sweetness and quality of the gold that had come out of the fire. I saw a picture in my spirit of Jesus reaching out to them in the wilderness and inviting them to leave it and walk out into a broad place of promise.

> WHILE CAPTIVITY IS A CONSEQUENCE OF JUDGMENT, WILDERNESS IS GOD'S PREPARATION FOR RESTORATION.

We don't choose seasons of wilderness—God does. Things can be going along smoothly, when all of a sudden the rug gets pulled out from beneath you; a loved one dies, a friend betrays you, you lose your job, you lose your hope or your sense of purpose in life. You find yourself in a new and unwanted place, trying to find your footing, trying to get back to "normal." But returning to normal isn't the goal of the wilderness; being transformed into the image of Jesus is the goal.

While captivity is a consequence of judgment, wilderness is God's preparation for restoration.

## MY WILDERNESS

I unknowingly followed the Lord into such a wilderness season in 1998. After an exhilarating but exhausting season of ministry in Dallas, Texas, I prepared to move back to San Jose, California, where I worked with Ed Silvoso as a city-reaching missionary.

I felt the Lord begin to deal with me about some things. I sensed the Lord asking me during one of my prayer times to lay my ministry at Harvest Evangelism on the "altar." It startled me, because this was the ministry to which the Lord had led me. My destiny was in city reaching, and the journey leading up to joining this ministry had been long and hard. So what did God want? Then I remembered how God asked Abraham to lay Isaac, the long-awaited promise, on the altar and give him to the Lord. When God saw that Abraham was willing to sacrifice Isaac, He put a ram in the bushes as the *real* sacrifice and gave Isaac back to Abraham.

Relieved and encouraged by this biblical precedent, I thought surely this is what the Lord was asking of me! So I wholeheartedly laid my ministry on the altar before the Lord. After I had done that, I heard the Lord quietly speak to me, "Don't count on My giving this back to you," and I knew in that moment it was gone. I can't quite explain how I knew, but I knew. *There was no going back.* The Lord had accepted my "willing" sacrifice.

As the reality of my decision sank in over the days and then weeks that followed, I felt that my life was over as far as I was concerned. My reputation (Who in their right mind leaves an international ministry like Harvest Evangelism?), my finances (How do you raise missionary support when you don't know what you're doing?), and my ministry vision were now in jeopardy (Where do I go?). I felt like an orphan.

After working through the transition and resigning from the ministry, I spent the summer in prayer, worship, and crying out to God. Some of it was nice and spiritual. Some of it was pathetic and ugly. I thought God had made a mistake. I told Him, "You are picking on the wrong person; there must be a mix-up in heaven." I reminded the Lord of the sacrifices I had made and all the things I had already done for Him. After all, hadn't I sold everything I owned *twice*? Hadn't I served him as a missionary in *another country*? Hadn't I left my family and friends and moved to California? Didn't those things *count*? Although I had been obedient to the Lord and joyfully followed His leading in my life, when the storm came, I wanted the equity to count; I wanted God to relent. I wanted my life back, and I wanted it all to make sense again.

Unknowingly, however, I was entering the world of "personal transformation." Not because I was in sin or had serious character issues, but because of something Jesus feels strongly about: our "being conformed into *His* image." That was new territory for me. I didn't have a paradigm for the wilderness and brokenness. So, in my ignorance, I concluded God was mad at me; I had somehow disappointed Him, and I was being punished.

The Lord laid my heart out before Him. Somewhere in the middle of the journey I had a revelation: The Lord wasn't after my ministry—He wanted my whole life!

I had been trying to reconcile His goodness and character with how I felt He was relating to me at the moment. I had no grid for "being conformed" through pain and loss. My early understanding was that He was trying to take things away from me. I realized later that He was actually trying to give me life. Then I had another revelation: He doesn't want to rearrange my life; He is really out to "kill" me! During my summer in the wilderness with Jesus, He challenged my ambitions, my motivations, my pride, and most of all, my identity. He began to separate out who I was from what I wanted to do for Him.

One day I reached the end of my rope. I was miserable, and a breakthrough was nowhere in sight; the Lord had removed several things that really mattered to me. In addition, I had run out of finances, had no clear direction, and, worst of all, I had no control. So I "fired" God. I told Him I was done with ministry and sacrificing myself to serve Him. Obviously He hadn't appreciated it very much, since I felt like He was being mean and unfair to me. I remember throwing up my hands and shouting at God, "Okay, I surrender." Something inside me just gave up the struggle for my old life; I stopped resisting the work God was doing in me. I lay on the floor exhausted and totally hopeless. He had won. I didn't know what He even wanted, really, but He had won. Then I heard a quiet voice speak in my spirit, saying, "That's all I ever wanted." It startled me. I had come to the end of myself and that's what He wanted? What did that mean??

Then something deep inside me connected. I found Jesus at the very bottom of the pit where I was now sitting. When everything else was stripped away, there He was, waiting for me. And there I was! There was more to me than I had realized, and the deep part of my spirit began to respond to God, free from the hindrances of a performance spirit and ministry trappings. It was just me and Jesus. It was the sweetest moment of my life.

## HIS STRENGTH IN OUR WEAKNESS

That fall I began traveling and ministering in cities again. Although I would share a bit about city transformation, the Lord began to use my testimony as the main message. I remember the first time the Lord prompted me to tell them the story of my journey into the wilderness with Him. I panicked; how could I share something so personal and transparent in public? He insisted, and quietly urged me by His Spirit to ignore my pride and share my story. I reluctantly shared that weekend in front of hundreds of people, my journey through the wilderness into personal transformation.

I'll never forget the response as people came to the altars and God moved in power to touch them and bring healing. I realized then how little ministers share their real stories and personal weaknesses. My transparency helped the people relate to the message at such a deep level that it allowed the Lord to meet them in that place and take them further.

The world is looking for life; they are looking for something real. I am always surprised how much people enjoy hearing my personal story of brokenness. People love to hear what a mess I was and how weak I still am. It's so encouraging to them! Why? Because it's true about all of us; we just don't admit it. It gives us hope to know we can be real and honest and that Jesus really is big enough to make something out of our lives in spite of ourselves.

There is a joy in realizing our weakness! Why? Because it means that Jesus himself will be perfected in our weakness if we offer it to Him. That is *so much* more exciting to me than trying to pretend I am something that I'm not. There is also tremendous freedom as we find victory in our weakness. Paul understood this principle well. He said,

> I was with you in weakness, in fear, and in much trembling. And my speech and my preaching were not with persuasive words of human wisdom, but in demonstration of the Spirit and of power, that your faith should not be in the wisdom of men but in the power of God. (1 Corinthians 2:3–5)
>
> Brothers, think of what you were when you were called. Not many of you were wise by human standards; not many were influential; not many were of noble birth. But God chose the foolish things of the world to shame the wise; God chose the weak things of the world to shame the strong. He chose the lowly things of this world and the despised things—and the things that are not—to

nullify the things that are, so that no one may boast before Him. (1
Corinthians 1:26–29 NIV)

It's wiser to embrace the wilderness season than to walk around
and around the mountain in an attempt to avoid pain. Why did Israel
wander around the wilderness for forty years? It was a journey of only
a few days from Egypt to the Promised Land. God wasn't teaching
them a geography lesson when he took them the long way around.
He was dealing with their hearts, to remove all the traces of Egypt in
preparation for the Promised Land.

We are called to become "living epistles," i.e., our life message is
developed through our journey in God and becomes what people
"read" when they meet us. What is the message people see in our
lives?

## PERSONAL TRANSFORMATION

We cannot hope to transform a city until the hearts of God's
people are transformed into the likeness of Jesus! Revival begins with
us as individuals and then we become carriers of God's life and glory
into our community.

We must be conformed to the image of Jesus and lay down our
appetites for the things of this world. We need a radical realignment
with God's holiness and kingdom in our own lives before we can
attempt to impact our cities. The issue isn't about having *enough*
Christians to do kingdom business; rather, the issue is finding Christians who have pressed through the fire and now look, talk, and smell
like Jesus!

Second Corinthians 3:18 says, "But we all, with unveiled face,
beholding as in a mirror the glory of the Lord, are being transformed
into the same image from glory to glory, just as by the Spirit of the
Lord." He is calling us to go from glory to glory. If the church isn't
beholding Jesus, she has no hope of becoming like Him. John says,
"And we beheld His glory" (1:14). Jesus wants us to behold His glory
and be transformed by it. The more we see Him, the more transformed we will be.

The wilderness seasons with God expose in us the places of hesitation or the places we want to keep from Him. He wants our hearts
fully, with no distance, no barriers, and no fear.

Glory inside must be released because you *are* the message; the work Jesus is doing inside you is what the world will see. They want something real and relevant, not something religious. We must become "living epistles" (2 Cor. 3:2). Colossians 1:27 says, "Christ *in* you, the hope of glory" (emphasis added). As you become transparent, the glory and nature of Jesus can be seen by those around you, and they will be drawn by His glory and fragrance.

The transformation of a city begins with the transformation of the church. Only revived, passionate believers can effect a spiritual revolution in their city. We must be transformed first! Once we are transformed, we can become carriers of His glory and releasers of His life into our communities. We can only minister out of an overflow or an abundance of what is going on inside of us. The church's attempt to evangelize or transform our city is futile if we have not been personally revived and transformed. We must become like Jesus or the city won't recognize the church as His bride.

What the Lord is doing *inside* of you has everything to do with what He can release *outside* of you! We are to become living epistles, life messages of His grace and love that can be "read" by the people around us. God has a purpose in refining us! It's for His glory: "Behold, I have refined you, but not as silver; I have tested you in the furnace of affliction. For My own sake, for My own sake, I will do it; for how should My name be profaned? And I will not give My glory to another" (Isa. 48:10–11).

## DANGER OF DISCONNECTION

One of the most serious issues we have as believers is the tendency to disconnect what is going on *inside* of us from what is happening on the *outside* of us. We compartmentalize our internal life as something separate from our external life and thus disconnect from reality. Ministry should be an

THE TRANSFORMATION OF A CITY BEGINS WITH THE TRANSFORMATION OF THE CHURCH.

overflow of the river of living water that flows out of your inmost being! If the water isn't fresh or flowing inside, what are we ministering out of? Sadly this is just the point—we continue to minister but out of our fleshly nature or human programs.

Jesus is looking for those who will press through the fire into personal revival and be filled with His glory and conformed to His image. Therefore, we must not compartmentalize and separate our *internal life* from our *external ministry*. If we do, we become shallow and double-minded, and therefore unstable, giving opportunity for the enemy to accuse and condemn us.

After committing adultery with Bathsheba, David wrote, "You desire truth in the inward parts, and in the hidden part You will make me to know wisdom" (Ps. 51:6). He went on to write in verse 17: "The sacrifices of God are a broken spirit, a broken and a contrite heart—these, O God, You will not despise." A broken and contrite heart is irresistible to the Lord!

Chapter 9

# RETURNING TO COVENANT

"I WILL BETROTH YOU TO ME FOREVER; I WILL
BETROTH YOU IN RIGHTEOUSNESS AND JUSTICE,
IN LOVE AND COMPASSION. I WILL BETROTH YOU
IN FAITHFULNESS, AND YOU WILL
ACKNOWLEDGE THE LORD."

HOSEA 2:19–20 NIV

People who have followed the Lord into a place of quietness and made it through the wilderness successfully have made right choices. Rather than becoming bitter from the testing, they have responded to God's invitation to be transformed. They have endured the testing of their heart, realized their spiritual poverty, and now possess a new level of dependence upon Jesus. They have learned to lean on Jesus in their weakness. Humility begins to replace the old pride and independence, and greater dependence upon the Lord produces a greater desperation for His continued presence.

## LEANING ON JESUS

We don't leave the wilderness season with the Lord confident in ourselves; we leave limping and maybe a bit uncertain. Sometimes the only thing we are confident in after a season of transformation with Jesus is an increased awareness of how weak we are but how strong He is! In the wilderness is where we realize we can lean on

Him. We see this picture in the Song of Solomon: "Who is this coming up from the wilderness, leaning upon her beloved?" (8:5).

I had an encounter with the Lord during a challenging ministry situation that caused me to lean on Jesus in a new way. Within hours of arriving at this conference I began to seriously question my decision to participate; my hosts had misrepresented several things to me, and nothing was going as planned. Because I had sacrificed several things in order to serve them at this event, I began struggling with my attitude about being there. As my frustration grew, I started turning over my thoughts to the Lord, asking for His help. This soon became a minute-by-minute conversation! I suspected that the Lord was deliberately offending my heart to allow these ugly things to surface so He and I could process them together. I confessed to the Lord that if I only traveled that far to encounter Him in a deeper way, then I would be satisfied despite the strange circumstances I found myself in. The Lord began to minister to me, and I felt like I was out in the wilderness with Jesus. Those two days were, in the end, two of the sweetest days I have spent with Him. He was right there, cleansing my heart, forgiving me, and helping me to mature.

I concluded that in my weak spiritual condition (which the Lord had gently but determinedly pointed out to me), I was totally unworthy to speak at the conference. But, of course, once I got to that point, I became "qualified" to minister. According to Paul in 1 Corinthians 1:27, "God has chosen the foolish things of the world to put to shame the wise, and God has chosen the weak things of the world to put to shame the things which are mighty." In the end the Lord used me to deliver a powerful message, and people encountered the Lord in a life-changing way. I didn't preach with "persuasive words of human wisdom, but in demonstration of the Spirit and of power" (1 Cor. 2:4) that my weakness qualified me for!

What was funny was that first night I pulled a muscle in my right hip, and I got up the next morning literally limping. I limped through the conference, all the way through the airport on my way home, and for several days afterward. It was confirmation to me that I had wrestled with God, and it was a good reminder of my dependence upon Him. I felt like Jacob after he wrestled with the Lord and was left with a limp as a reminder of his personal transformation!

## COMPASSION AND RESTORATION

We may be painfully aware of our unfaithfulness and our weakness, but if we offer ourselves to Jesus and allow Him to transform us, He begins to perfect himself in us. Then we can say with Paul that it is no longer I but Christ who lives in me (Galatians 2:20). Therefore, we are no longer ashamed of our condition. We may feel weak, *but at least we are leaning!*

We need to understand that God loves us even in our weakness and proneness to wander, and whatever correction He may bring to our hearts is gentle and full of love. Rather than finding disappointment in His eyes, we will find His deep longing for us, a love so intense and so perfect that we struggle to trust it.

The Lord's response to our condition is the same as His response to Israel, as we see in the book of Hosea. He responds to her spiritual adultery with compassion and mercy. After He allures her into the wilderness, away from her preoccupations, to speak tenderly to her He offers,

> "I will give her her vineyards from there, and the Valley of Achor as a door of hope; she shall sing there, as in the days of her youth, as in the day when she came up from the land of Egypt" (Hosea 2:15).

The Lord is promising to restore her in several ways. First, He promises to restore her fruitfulness by giving her back her vineyards. Then He says that the Valley of Achor will become a door of hope to her. The word *Achor* can also be translated "trouble" (this was the valley where they stoned Achan for stealing and hiding the treasure in his tent). The Lord is promising to bring her out of her trouble through a door called *hope.*

He also promises to restore her joy; "she shall sing *there,* as in the days of her youth," as in the Exodus from Egypt. That is speaking of the time when she first became free, released from the bondages of Pharaoh and taken out into a wilderness of testing and purifying. It began as a journey of rejoicing in their newfound freedom; now He is restoring to her that same joy.

*There is a door of hope in the valley of trouble!* As long as there is a generation that loves the King, there is hope. As long as there are those who long for His beauty, there is hope. As long as there are those willing to pay the price for His presence, there is hope. And as long as there are weak, wandering people who long to be married to a faithful Bridegroom, there is hope!

## RETURNING TO COVENANT

After promising restoration of fruitfulness, joy, hope, and freedom the passage in Hosea continues by promising the ultimate restoration: God himself. God offers the wandering bride the promise of covenant betrothal:

> "In that day," declares the Lord, "you will call me 'my husband,' you will no longer call Me 'my master'" (Hosea 2:16 NIV).

He continues a couple of verses later:

> "I will betroth you to me forever; I will betroth you in righteousness and justice, in love and compassion. I will betroth you in faithfulness, and you will acknowledge the Lord" (Hosea 2:19–20 NIV).

What kind of love is it that would willingly trade adultery for betrothal? God not only called her away to speak tenderly to her, He also covered her shame with righteousness, justice, love, and compassion. God doesn't lick His wounds and seek revenge. Instead, *He shows us His beauty, draws us away with Him, and reminds us of His love.* He delights in turning our wandering hearts back to faithfulness.

God's objective in this story of Hosea is to bring a rejected, shame-filled, adulterous bride back under His protective care—to give her "beauty for ashes" and "the oil of joy for mourning" (Isa. 61:3).

God is a "jealous" husband in a pure and redemptive sense. He is a covenant maker and a covenant keeper! God is not looking for fleeting relationships but for covenant relationships that have permanence and purpose.

## COVENANT WITH GOD

When God initiated a relationship with mankind, He did it by inviting Abraham into a covenant relationship. This covenant was to bring blessing and ultimately redemption to the nations. The covenant involved a promise of an heir for Abraham, an inheritance in the land, and a heritage of many descendents. Ultimately, this covenant promised a "seed" that would come through Abraham that would provide a Redeemer for mankind, Jesus Christ.

The fundamental promise of this covenant is the promise of God in Genesis 12:1–3. Then in Genesis 17:7, He states, "I will establish My covenant as an everlasting covenant between Me and you and your descendants after you in their generations, for an everlasting covenant, to be God to you and your descendants after you." All the other covenant promises derive from this covenant. It means that God binds himself to His people to be their God and to grant them His grace, goodness, protection, and blessing. The first redemptive covenant God established was with Abraham.

God has made it clear in His word that He wants to relate to us in covenant. He wants personal, intimate relationship that includes commitment. Covenant in God's eyes is irrevocable, as in a marriage covenant. It is a serious commitment that may not be broken; it's a pledge of love, loyalty, faithfulness, and devotion.

God has entered into a blood covenant with humanity that is irrevocable and eternal. What God demonstrated through the sacrificial system of the old covenant became the new covenant in Christ Jesus. There has been a final "blood sacrifice." The ultimate price has been paid for our redemption and fellowship with God by Jesus' sacrifice on the cross.

## MAKING COVENANT

In ancient times it was common for people to enter into agreements with one another through the ceremony of covenant. Covenant is simply an arrangement between two parties with specific and mutual obligations to be fulfilled. It's a binding agreement that requires a commitment to responsibility and action.

In his book *The Covenant* Ames Garlow shares a number of steps involved in the covenant-making ceremony that symbolized the participants' mutual commitment to each other. As a part of the ceremony, for example, a number of things were exchanged between the two parties, thus making them "one." The first thing they would exchange was their robes or outer garments to represent an exchange of *identity*. The second exchange was their belts, which held their military gear; this represented the *sharing of strength and assets*. Yet another step in the ceremony was the exchange of weapons, which symbolized the *exchange of enemies*. This meant that your enemies are now my enemies, and vice versa.

The fourth step involved the sacrifice of an animal, thus making it a *"blood covenant"* and forever binding. Life had to be given, and therefore blood had to be shed, in order to make the covenant binding.

Finally, they *exchanged names* by inserting the other party's name in the middle of their own. This meant that every time their new name was spoken it would tell people who their covenant partner was. This is what God did with Abraham. His name was Abram, and God added His own name, "AH," which comes from Yahweh, and he became AbrAHam. God also took Abraham's name. Time after time in Scripture God refers to himself as "the God of Abraham." *Attached to God's name is the name of a man—His covenant partner.*[1]

## TWO TYPES OF COVENANT TREATIES

There were two kinds of treaties in biblical times that served as types of covenant agreements. First there was the "parity" treaty, which was a covenant made between two people. It was called a "parity" treaty because this covenant was an exchange between two equal parties. They would exchange assets and strengths equally and bind themselves together in the agreement.

The second type of treaty or covenant was the "suzerainty" treaty. This was the type of treaty in which a king, who possessed everything, would enter into a covenant with a peasant, who possessed nothing. The covenant God binds himself to with man is obviously not a parity treaty but a suzerain treaty!

Think of God introducing himself to us this way:

> *I want to enter into a covenant with you. I want to give you*
> *everything I have, I want to exchange your identity for My identity,*
> *I want your enemies to be My enemies and for My name to be your*
> *name. I want this to be a lasting covenant for eternity. I want to*
> *give you My nature, all the resources of heaven, and give you an*
> *inheritance not only in this life but also in the life to come.*

"But I don't have anything to give to you in return!" we reply.

"I know," the Lord responds.

"All I have to give to you is *me,* my love, my loyalty," we explain.

"That's all I ever wanted, and it's exactly what I'm asking for," says the Lord.[2]

That's what the Lord is asking of us—to love Him, to bind ourselves to Him as He has bound himself to us in covenant relationship. It's a covenant that Jesus made possible through His death on the cross. It cost Him everything; we paid nothing. How can we refuse such love or treat it as something less than it is?

## COVENANT WITH EACH OTHER

We must first be restored to the covenant relationship with God that He provides for us through His Son, Jesus Christ. We enter into that covenant not only individually but as a corporate body. For too long the church has been fragmented, independent, and individualistic. As a result we have failed to recognize our need for each other as members of the same family and household of God.

We struggle with this concept in the Western world in relationship to commitment; we commit more out of emotions and then back out if it becomes inconvenient, takes too long, or is too labor intensive. We like everything to have quick results and to meet our needs immediately. But relationships without covenant commitment result in much pain and brokenness. Covenant is about relationship with long-term commitment, believing in one another and walking it out together. Covenant relationship provides security; there is no security without covenant.

Covenant means a mutual commitment and responsibility on the part of God to us and us to God. Horizontally, it means that with one another, we in the body are agreeing with God's purposes. Covenant is an irrevocable commitment, not a temporary relationship based on convenience.

Remember the covenant friendship between David and Jonathan? It says that "the soul of Jonathan was knit to the soul of David, and Jonathan loved him as his own soul" (1 Sam. 18:1). They exchanged garments, armor and belt, and enemies, thus becoming full covenant partners. As a result of that covenant friendship, David sought out the crippled son of Jonathan long after Jonathan's death, to "show him kindness for Jonathan's sake" (2 Sam. 9:1). Covenant is meant to be multigenerational and long lasting.

Unfortunately, many of us are more likely to operate according to a "trade alliance" mentality than a sense of covenant with each other. We make decisions based on who can meet our needs at the moment, functioning according to a value based on expediency— whatever seems advantageous for the moment—which is the antithesis of covenant. We have become transient and temporary people, moving from place to place according to opportunity. We have also become shortsighted, operating on short-term advantages rather than long-range commitments.

It's important for us to realize that if we aren't in covenant with God, with each other, and with the land where God has placed us, there cannot be fruitfulness. Long-lasting, legitimate fruitfulness can only come through covenant and intimacy. Superficial relationships based on personal agendas produce mere rhetoric and busyness. Only God's Spirit can produce life; and He breathes on those things that are in agreement with His covenant promises, conditions, and relationships.

## COVENANT WITH THE LAND

One of the core elements of God's covenant with His people is His promise to give them land as their inheritance. It began in the Garden of Eden when Adam and Eve were given the responsibility of subduing the land and caring for it, both to meet their own needs and also to glorify God. But when Adam and Eve sinned, the land became cursed and they were forced to labor and provide for themselves.

In the Abrahamic covenant, the Lord told Abraham to go "to a land that I will show you" (Gen. 12:1). The land of Canaan was an important part of God's covenantal promises to Abraham. God had promised Abraham blessed land as his inheritance! The land is described as fruitful (Deuteronomy 8:7–10; 11:10–12). This was a place where God's people would find prosperity and blessing. This connection between covenant obedience and the land is repeated in the book of Joshua (1:3, 6, 11, 13).

In Isaiah 62, the Lord makes it clear that He longs to draw His people back into covenant relationship with Him, and He describes this in terms of the covenant of marriage: "For the Lord will take delight in you, and your land will be married. As a young man marries a maiden, so will your sons marry you; as a bridegroom rejoices over his bride, so will your God rejoice over you" (Isa. 62:4–5 NIV).

In this passage, the Lord is not only speaking to His people about covenant but also of the land they live in; He says that the very land will be "married." Why? Because when people are restored to covenant with God, those promises and blessings always include land. It's not just a spiritual concept—God literally wants to bring restoration and healing to the communities we live in. When the people of God were obedient, they were blessed!

Take, for example, Deuteronomy 28. Here the Lord describes the blessings and promises He makes to His people when they obey His Word and keep His covenant:

> "Blessed shall be the fruit of your body, the produce of your ground and the increase of your herds" (v. 4).
>
> "The Lord will command the blessing on you in your storehouses and in all to which you set your hand, and He will bless you in the land which the Lord your God is giving you" (v. 8).

By contrast, when people rebelled against God through disobedience or unbelief they were removed from their land. The land itself was cursed because of sin (Leviticus 18:25), or they were not allowed to enter their rest (Hebrews 3:9–11).

Ultimately, God is going to create a new heaven and a new earth. He intends to bring restoration to creation—literally. What we see happening in transformed communities is just a glimpse of the restoration God has in mind. When a community is life-giving, restored by God's presence, and serves as a blessing to people, it brings Him glory. A devastated city, full of spiritual and natural decay and poverty, on the other hand, glorifies the work of the enemy.

## RETURNING TO GOD'S COVENANT INVITATION

The church has all too often chosen to relate to God superficially. She has broken or neglected covenant vows and has generally been unfaithful to God, much like Israel in the book of Hosea. We must remember that we can't relate to God on our terms; we don't make the covenant agreements and we can't negotiate with God about them. Instead, we are expected to walk in obedient faith in order to see the fulfillment of the promise and blessing contained in God's covenant with us.

In 2 Chronicles 7:14, God promises, "If My people who are called by My name will humble themselves, and pray and seek My face, and turn from their wicked ways, then I will hear from heaven, and will forgive their sin and *heal their land.*" This verse is set in the context of Solomon dedicating the temple to the Lord and agreeing to live in a covenant relationship with Him as a faithful people. God responds by stating the conditions of their relationship; if the people do their part, God will fulfill His. An important part of God's promise to them is the healing of their land.

The people in the Hebrides Revival understood the issue of covenant. The promise in 2 Chronicles 7:14 became a focus for their intercession before God on behalf of their community. They knew and understood that if they fulfilled their obligation in the covenant to (1) humble themselves; (2) pray and seek God's face; and (3) turn from their wicked ways, then God would also fulfill His part of the covenant to (1) hear their prayer; (2) forgive their sin; and (3) heal their land. And that's exactly what happened!

The tremendous promise found in 2 Chronicles 7:14 is being lived out today in hundreds of communities around the world. Believers are humbling themselves, praying, and seeking God, returning to covenant relationship with Him and with each other. We are watching as God responds to their cry in powerful, supernatural ways. He is listening, He is forgiving, and in many cases He is healing not only the people but also land—restoring it to life and abundance for His glory.

The promises of God are always related to covenant relationship. That means that in God's eyes they are irrevocable and real and He can be trusted to fulfill them. When we live in covenant relationship with God and each other our lives will be blessed. And when we pray for our communities out of that covenant relationship our prayer will take on a reality that is not wishful thinking, because we are praying according to God's eternal agenda, not our temporal perspective.

## ARE WE WILLING TO COMMIT TO OUR CITY?

God wants to give us territory in our cities and nations so His kingdom will be accomplished on earth as it is in heaven. If you are living an obedient life with the Lord, then the place where you are living is by His design. You didn't get there by accident or mistake! God has brought you to the city or community where you live for a purpose (Jeremiah 29:7, 11–13). Once we accept our responsibility to be a blessing where He has planted our feet, we can fulfill our calling and destiny in it.

The question is, are we committing to the city where we live or are we just living in it to fulfill our own purposes? When you commit yourself to your city for God's kingdom purpose, you commit to love the people in it, to serve them as long as the Lord has called you to be there. You won't move after three or four years to another location if a "greater opportunity" arises, unless the Lord has released you from your current spiritual "assignment" to commit to another one.

Land is important to God. Paul states, "And He has made from one blood every nation of men to dwell on all the face of the earth, and has determined their preappointed times and the boundaries of their habitation." He continues with this instruction: "so that they should seek the Lord, in the hope that they might grope for Him and find Him, though He is not far from each one of us" (Acts 17:26–27).

This is an important issue for leaders who have a heart for transforming their cities. Often when I am talking to leaders about their cities, we begin to talk about God's heart for covenant with the city. Leaders often confess that they have never considered God's covenant promises for their city. I have watched God break their hearts for their city and connect their heart to God's heart. Powerful breakthroughs often occur as a result of deepening our understanding and commitment to what and where God has called us to serve Him.

And if we aren't in covenant with God for the land of our inheritance, why should we expect Him to give us fruitfulness (see Colossians 1:9–10)? You can't have real intimacy without covenant, and you can't have fruitfulness without intimacy.

Jesus said that the gospel must be spread to the ends of the earth and then the end will come (Matthew 24:14). That means that the testimony of Jesus and His glory will cover the earth. It will touch real people living and working in real places!

## HOPE FOR HAITI—A TESTIMONY OF RESTORED COVENANT

How can committing together in covenant relationship to God, to each other, and to a land make a difference? The following testimony is about a congregation who realized their responsibility to be covenant keepers with the Lord, relating to the land of their inheritance, with God, and with each other in order to possess their inheritance individually and corporately.

Until two hundred years ago, Haiti was known as the "Pearl of the Antilles" because it was the most beautiful island in the Caribbean. But two hundred years ago the people of Haiti made a pact with the devil that if he would deliver them from the oppression of the French, they would dedicate the country to him. The Haitians rose up, defeated the French, and gained their freedom after making their pact with Satan. The price for their covenant with Satan has been costly. Today the island is desolate and barren, its fishing industry has collapsed, and Haiti is now the poorest country in the Western hemisphere. The president recently announced that voodoo is the official religion of Haiti. But God hasn't given up on this nation!

Marvin and Sally Adams pastor River Community Church in Chicago and also are leaders of the Prayer Furnace, a citywide 24/7 prayer and worship ministry. In 1996, they adopted a young boy named James from an orphanage in Haiti. James has grown up to be a godly young man, now twenty years old. As he grew in the Lord, so did his heart for the nation of Haiti. He longs to see life come to the people of Haiti and for them to be delivered from the curse of voodoo and poverty. His dream has been to return and bring hope to the land of his heritage.

In the fall of 2003 James led a small team of passionate young people from Chicago to Haiti to minister in the orphanage and preach in churches. During the week of ministry, James was able to spend time with his younger brother Djecky (pronounced "Jakie"), who was still living in the orphanage and not doing well. The boy was malnourished and received regular beatings. Brokenhearted, James called home about his brother. The team longed to do something but didn't have the means. Marvin and Sally needed to come up with $5,000 to adopt Djecky, but it seemed impossible. They couldn't understand why God wasn't allowing them to adopt this little boy, and they grieved for James, who had to leave his brother in the orphanage.

The youth team returned from their trip to Haiti a couple of days before I traveled to Chicago to speak at a City Transformation Conference. The theme for the weekend was covenant, first to the Lord as our Bridegroom, then with each other as the body of Christ, and finally with the land of our inheritance.

Sunday morning as I prepared to minister in Marvin and Sally's congregation, I prayed and asked the Lord to give me His heart for the people. In my spirit I heard Him call them "people of purpose." Then the Lord said to me, "They are going on a treasure hunt," and He gave me the verse about searching for a pearl of great price (Matthew 13:46).

As James and his team got up and gave a brief testimony about their trip to Haiti, something broke inside my heart. When I saw this young man, talking about taking a team of young people *back* to the orphanage where *he* once lived and ministering to the people of his nation, I began to cry. The Lord broke my heart with His heart for Haiti and I heard Him ask a question: "Who will covenant with Haiti? Who will bring her hope?"

I stood up to preach but had difficulty focusing on a clear message because my heart was gripped by God regarding the nation of Haiti. As I began to share about the issue of covenant, James began praying quietly, asking the Lord to give him his nation as his inheritance. Then the Lord turned my attention to James, and I began to speak to him.

"James, the Lord says Haiti is yours if you want it," I said. He began to weep. Many in the congregation were weeping by that time too. The next thing I heard coming out of my mouth was, "Whatever you ask of the Lord for your nation, He will give you. Haiti is your inheritance!" Then I asked him a question: "How many orphanages do you want?" I learned later that James and his fiancée, Tabitha, had been asking the Lord to plant an orphanage in Haiti.

As I spoke, the Lord shared His desire that they as a people "adopt" Haiti. What was happening? My heart was stirred, but my mind couldn't process it quickly enough. Next I shared that the Lord said they were on a "treasure hunt," and I referred to the parable of the "pearl of great price" and how we must be willing to give everything we have to possess the treasure. Little did I know then that Haiti had been called the "Pearl of the Antilles."

When I finished ministering, Marvin got up to the podium, weeping. The Lord had told him clearly that the reason they couldn't adopt Djecky was because He wanted the congregation to be involved—Marvin and Sally weren't to adopt him by themselves. Then I saw what was happening. The whole morning was about agreeing with God's heart to covenant with this devastated nation. He was inviting the congregation to adopt Djecky as a symbolic first step—he became a symbol of covenant and promise!

All of a sudden people began bringing money to the podium and handing it to their pastor, who stood there stunned. A flood of giving began and a sense of joy and purpose filled the congregation as we prayed for the nation of Haiti together.

The ushers returned with news of the offering. It totaled $6,900. I just sat there speechless. By the time we left the church, it had increased to $8,600, and two days later the adoption offering totaled more than $10,000! People kept giving even after they knew the required amount had been met. The people of River Community had found their purpose, and it included a young man, a broken nation, and an inheritance that they are to share with Jesus.

Two days after that Sunday morning service, James spoke on the phone with his uncle in Haiti, who is heavily involved in voodoo. He told James about his desire to meet Jesus, saying that Jesus had been tugging on his heart for many years. He also told James he had a little plot of land in Haiti that he would like to give to James to build a church, an orphanage, or a house of prayer!

Marvin reported several months later that God has turned his congregation upside down. The whole church focus is now directed to two things: establishing day-and-night worship and intercession and ministering to the nation of Haiti. The church is growing, financial breakthroughs continue, and people are willing to make huge sacrifices for the purpose and destiny the Lord has given them. They have become a corporate "people of purpose."

Is there *any* reason why Haiti cannot be transformed? Of course not! Haiti not only desperately needs spiritual, social, and political transformation, but the people also desperately need their barren land to be restored to life and fruitfulness. God longs to restore Haiti to her former beauty and fruitful condition so that He can be glorified and His people blessed.

Shortly after God called these people to covenant with Him on behalf of the land of Haiti, the nation erupted in violence and President Aristide was removed from office; this nation is being contended for! I believe these recent events are birth pangs of a breakthrough, which will lead to the healing and restoration of a forsaken and desolate place. Even in the midst of the violence and uncertainty, teams are traveling to Haiti to pray, worship, and build a dwelling place for God's presence in the midst of desperation. When God finds faithful people, He will accomplish His purposes. He will build His church and the gates of hell will not prevail against it.

## POSSESSING OUR INHERITANCE

While there are exceptions, much of the church is totally unaware of the importance of committing to the area where they live if they are going to see long-lasting spiritual results. What does that look like in your community? What about the institutions of city government or education? God longs to heal the community wherever it needs restoration. He doesn't have a pat answer that He applies universally to every location. We must identify what is desolate and forsaken, both spiritually and physically, and respond to the Lord according to 2 Chronicles 7:14, trusting Him to bring restoration.

Depending upon the sphere of influence God has given you, you may be called to bring hope and healing to a classroom of students, an office of co-workers, or your neighborhood. But if you *live* in your city, you have a rightful inheritance and responsibility to *affect* it with God's love and His glory! God is issuing the same invitation to us today that He offered to rebellious Israel: Return to your first love and step through the Door of Hope!

# DOOR OF HEAVEN

"After these things I looked, and behold, a door standing open in heaven. And the first voice which I heard was like a trumpet speaking with me, saying, 'Come up here, and I will show you things which must take place after this.'"

REVELATION 4:1

## Chapter 10

# RESTORATION OF THE PRIESTHOOD

"YOU ALSO, AS LIVING STONES ARE BEING BUILT
UP A SPIRITUAL HOUSE, A HOLY PRIESTHOOD, TO
OFFER UP SPIRITUAL SACRIFICES ACCEPTABLE TO
GOD THROUGH JESUS CHRIST."

1 PETER 2:5

"Jesus! Save our city!" one pastor cried out. "Let Your kingdom come to our city!" another prayed. One by one, leaders made their requests to the Lord on behalf of their city. We were all gripped by God's presence in the room. There was no question in our minds that the Lord was listening to us. It felt like we had a direct line to heaven, and every word raised up to the Lord was heard in the throne room. Some began to weep and plead with the Lord for the children of the city; others cried out with concern for the high divorce rate among police officers; others made requests on behalf of families, for the economy, and for the people of the city to be saved.

We were gathered for a citywide pastors' and leaders' meeting that Saturday morning in Anderson, Indiana. I had been asked to teach a brief seminar on transformation. About ten minutes before I was scheduled to speak, I sensed the Lord had something specific on His heart for the meeting, so I began to earnestly seek Him about what He wanted me to share. I longed for a fresh word from the Lord to encourage my friends.

As I prayed, the Lord prompted me with a verse from Nehemiah, where King Artaxerxes asks Nehemiah, "What is your request of Me?" (2:4). Nehemiah responds by telling him how he is burdened to return to rebuild the city of Jerusalem. The King promptly proceeds to give Nehemiah every resource and favor needed to go and rebuild the devastated city of Jerusalem. I sensed the Lord was asking the same question of the pastors gathered that morning: What was *their* request for their city?

I realized that if God wanted to hear their requests, it wasn't because He didn't already know what the city needed. It was because He wanted to *answer* the prayers of the spiritual gatekeepers who, like Nehemiah, were seeking the welfare of their city. God was not only listening to the prayers of these pastors, He was also about to respond!

I shared what I believed the Lord was inviting them to do, and one by one, leaders came up and began to pray to the Lord on behalf of their city. Pastor Johnny Cawthon was the last pastor to pray. He had been carefully listening and making notes about what had been prayed by the others and making a list of everything that hadn't yet been mentioned. When he stood up to the microphone, he said, "I want to make sure *everything* on the list is covered!"

A month later the mayor, who had heard the report of the prayer meeting, called for a second meeting at City Hall. He personally sent out invitations to the city department heads to encourage their attendance. The pastors, intercessors, and the media were also invited by the citywide pastors' network. At the meeting, a PowerPoint presentation was made that listed all the prayer requests that were being made on behalf of the city. A clear message was sent: The church of Anderson is praying for you!

The next morning that report made the front page of the newspaper! People in the city were encouraged (and undoubtedly a bit surprised) to find out that Christian believers were praying for their jobs, their children, their health, and the economy. Somebody was defending and fighting for them in prayer! The media in this city regularly covers the activities of the citywide church of Anderson not with cynicism or doubt but with friendly interest. They report what the citywide church is doing together, at times placing the report right on the front page of the newspaper.

The leaders in Anderson, Indiana, are doing exactly what the church of Jesus Christ is supposed to be doing—functioning as a priesthood for the needs of their city! God is raising up His priests in cities and nations to cry out to Him on behalf of their communities. He is calling us back to our primary job description as His people— to be ministers of reconciliation.

## CONTAGIOUS DESPERATION!

Fast-forward a couple of years. The transformation vision is now spreading and igniting hearts all over Indiana. A regional team of pastors from several cities began to meet together to seek the Lord's heart for their cities. As a result of this, they decided to host a transformation conference together in October 2003. This wasn't hosted by one congregation; it wasn't even hosted by a citywide pastors' network; they formed a unified team from *several cities* and hosted the conference together.

Although we had already sensed a real excitement in several communities, we were surprised to learn that sixty-seven churches were represented from forty-six cities and five states! The Lord had indeed "blown a trumpet" to gather people for this event!

The highlight of the conference was Friday evening, when we stopped worshiping about ten, and a hush came over the room. We all sat in *total* silence for about thirty minutes. It wasn't an empty silence; it was "pregnant" with purpose—we just didn't know what the purpose was yet! As we waited, we all sensed the Lord's presence like a thick blanket filling the room. Our hearts were pounding! George Otis Jr. sensed the Lord inviting the region into transformation and shared that with the people. We continued to worship until after eleven that night. We encountered the Lord powerfully during that weekend. He visited us and took us deeper into His heart both as individual believers and as community leaders. He stirred a deep hunger for more of His presence.

There were some amazing developments in the region as a result of our encounter with the Lord that weekend. Leaders reported a "holy disruption" of their normal routines following the conference, and they now feel a mandate from the Lord to connect with a larger vision for regional transformation. There is a great hunger to see cities unite and they believe that they have been given an invitation by Jesus to act upon it. Regional fasts have been called; pastors are being gathered to receive vision about the needs of their area, and unity within the body is growing.

What excites me most about what is happening in this region of Indiana is that it's grounded through friendship and organic unity. They don't have a plan or highly involved strategy. They aren't "peddling" their new successes or adopting the successes of others. They just want Jesus to come to their communities, and they are willing to seek Him and work toward that end together.

My friend Derek Loux, the director of the House of Prayer in Indianapolis, shared his perspective about the call to fasting and prayer this way: "The longing for His presence is just too great now, what else can we do but seek Him?"

## IMPACTING YOUR CITY THROUGH PRAYER

As we grow in understanding of our identity as the bride of Christ we are led deeper and deeper into the heart of Jesus, our Great High Priest. We are called to enter into the Holy of Holies and partner with Jesus in prayer concerning His plans and purposes on the earth.

Every person and every household must be connected to the power and love of God through prayer. Through priestly intercession and mediation, the whole church can minister to the whole city! Nobody should be able to live in a city where the church exists without coming into contact with Jesus through His body praying for them.

I had the privilege of working for several years with Ed Silvoso of Harvest Evangelism. Ed leads a city-reaching ministry focused on reaching entire cities through "prayer evangelism." Part of the strategy of prayer evangelism is to establish "lighthouses of prayer" around the city. These are homes or workplaces where believers are praying and caring for the people around them, looking for opportunities to minister in tangible ways. I became very involved in the Lighthouse of Prayer movement and had the opportunity to see city after city begin to pray for their neighbors regularly. We received countless testimonies of individuals who had turned their home or business into a lighthouse of prayer and saw the Lord respond in powerful ways. I remember a testimony of a six-year-old girl whose faithful prayer walking ministry around her neighborhood led to the salvation of an entire family—over thirty people!

The Lighthouse of Prayer movement has been effective in mobilizing the corporate body of Christ in a city to begin to pray for and care for the people within their sphere of influence. What we discovered is that if portions of the city were prayed for over a period of time, giving the Holy Spirit a chance to do His work in the hearts of people, whatever ministry that took place next was *much more effective*. We heard many times the testimony of other ministries that were so grateful that the city had lighthouses of prayer operating to cover the city in prayer before their outwardly focused ministry took place. Oswald Chambers once said, "Prayer isn't what you do before the work—prayer IS the work." Sustained fervent prayer should be the critical foundation for our ministry expressions into the city.

We must understand that our purpose as priests is to become a promoter of God's presence—that Jesus himself would be introduced into our neighborhoods. Our mission is to introduce the reality of who Jesus is in a tangible way to our friends, family, and co-workers. Our role as ministers of the gospel is to make room and opportunity for Jesus to touch people, not try to be the whole answer ourselves. How much room do we give Jesus? How much time?

> SUSTAINED FERVENT PRAYER SHOULD BE THE CRITICAL FOUNDATION FOR OUR MINISTRY EXPRESSIONS INTO THE CITY.

## PRIESTLY PURPOSE

We have the privilege and responsibility of being mediators before God on behalf of men and before men on behalf of God. While Jesus is the "Great High Priest" who lives to constantly make intercession for us in heaven, we join Him in His priestly function as mediators on the earth. We actually partner with the intercession of Jesus by agreeing with His heart and His mind.

Every person who has been born again and redeemed into God's family has become a member of what Paul refers to as "a royal priesthood" and "chosen generation" (1 Peter 2:9). This isn't a special calling for only a few but rather part of our identity as the bride of Christ.

We can understand our role as a priestly people only in light of the access to the Holy of Holies—God's presence—that Jesus provides for us through His death on the cross. The writer of Hebrews shares a powerful truth in chapter 4:14–16:

> Seeing then that we have a great High Priest who has passed through the heavens, Jesus the Son of God, let us hold fast our confession. For we do not have a High Priest who cannot sympathize with our weaknesses, but was in all points tempted as we are, yet without sin. Let us therefore come boldly to the throne of grace, that we may obtain mercy and find grace to help in time of need.

WE NEED TO MOVE PRAYER FROM A "CHURCH" ACTIVITY TO A "CITY" RESPONSIBILITY.

We can approach the throne of God with confidence because of the access Jesus has provided for us through His death and resurrection. Jesus is our High Priest forever, and we enter into our priestly function through Him. Prayer is not an activity, it's an expression of an intimate relationship with Christ Jesus. When we touch the heart of Jesus, we are connected to the infirmities, pain, and suffering of people around us. We begin to feel His heart and we are moved with compassion as we pray for others.

What would a city look like if every believer in the city was functioning as a spiritual gatekeeper and guarding the city through prayer? What if the hurting, broken people in the city were being fought for in prayer, had people standing in the gap on their behalf, fighting for them to be freed from darkness and despair? We need to move prayer from a "church" activity to a "city" responsibility.

## WHO ARE THE "WATCHMEN"?

To "watch" means to be alert, vigilant, and awake. In ancient times watchmen were those who stood guard on the protective walls of the city and communicated with the guards at the gates. If the watchmen saw friends approaching the city, they would call down to the guards, and the guards would open the gates and welcome the visitors. If, however, the watchmen saw an enemy approaching the city, they would alert the guards to lock the gates and arm themselves to protect the city against the enemy.

To "watch" in the spiritual sense is the same. We as the priesthood are given the privilege and responsibility to watch over our cities. Through prayer we discern the spiritual "traffic" approaching our city and then we take our place in prayer, agreeing with God's heart for what He is allowing to come into the city and what He wants us to defend our city against.

> I have set watchmen on your walls, O Jerusalem; they shall never hold their peace day or night. You who make mention of the Lord, do not keep silent, and give Him no rest till He establishes and till He makes Jerusalem a praise of the earth. (Isaiah 62:6–7)

The body of Christ has taken off her priestly robes of mediation and has abdicated her spiritual responsibility, leaving the people of our cities to fend for themselves. Contenting ourselves with merely "doing church," we have tragically left our cities defenseless against the attacks of the enemy. No matter what other good works we may be doing as we gather together in our church buildings, if we aren't praying, we aren't functioning in our roles as priests and mediators for men before God. The lost people in our cities and communities suffer when we are not obedient to our calling.

We need intercessors to set themselves as "watchmen" upon the walls of their cities, praying day and night, taking the responsibility for their cities, reminding God of His Word and covenant promises, and "[giving] Him no rest till He establishes [their cities] a praise in the earth" (Isa. 62:7). These watchmen stir God's heart and bring hope to their cities.

## WHO IS CONTROLLING THE SPIRITUAL THERMOSTAT?

Every city and community has a spiritual "climate." This can sometimes be felt by just driving into a community. There are places in our communities where you can sense in your spirit and see with your eyes the darkness, materialism, and poverty. There are also places where you can sense joy, freedom, and hope. This spiritual climate will be determined by the activity of the people of God in that community. The enemy is a trespasser and can only regulate and influence what has been given over to him. The church, on the other hand, is authorized to enforce the authority Jesus has given us to be victorious over the enemy in our communities.

Cities don't have demilitarized zones; they will either be filled with the kingdom of God or with strongholds of the enemy. When we have not taken our places in prayer and ministry in the city, a spiritual vacuum results and, like a cavity, starts rotting and decaying, going from bad to worse. The question is: Who is going to fill the vacuum? The kingdom that fills the vacuum is going to regulate the spiritual climate of the city. Who will set the central thermostat?

I saw a clear illustration of this principle one summer when I was ministering in south central Los Angeles. I was participating in a children's outreach every Saturday in a local community park. This particular location was disputed gang territory, and several gangs, including the "Crips" and the "Bloods," were fighting over this block regularly. Gun fights, prostitution, and child abuse were common. Fear was the prevailing reality of the neighborhood.

When I became involved in the ministry, I started to lead prayer walks around the park. A couple of us would walk around the entire perimeter of the neighborhood where we would be ministering, praying for God's protection, His presence to come, and His purposes to be fulfilled in the lives of the children and their parents that day. We also asked the Lord to set that neighborhood aside for His Spirit; we declared the kingdom of God as the ruling and governing reality while we were there.

It was amazing the things that would happen as a result. This dangerous neighborhood would be transformed into a sanctuary of God's presence on Saturdays! Although gang members and prostitutes would hang out across the street, we didn't have any incidents in the park or in the community center where we were teaching. Quite the opposite! We watched the Lord minister to hundreds of hurting families as we made friends with the people in the neighborhood, visiting them, bringing them food, and caring for their children.

As the ministry continued, the reputation of the "church" in the neighborhood spread. The gangs came to respect the ministry, calling it "church," which meant they would show it respect. This was important because it caused them to consider the community park off limits for gang activity on Saturdays until the afternoon ministry time was completed.

You could feel a distinct change when you stepped off the block of the community park and crossed the street into the neighborhood. It was like walking out of light and into darkness. You could also feel the same thing happening in the community park when the ministry packed up and left for the day. By 5:00 P.M. the community park reverted back to its original state.

## RESTORATION OF SPIRITUAL RESPONSIBILITY

We must put our priestly garments back on and take back the spiritual responsibility we have relinquished to civil authority and social systems. We must begin to function as the priesthood of believers in our communities. God is longing to restore the functioning priesthood. When we pray, we touch heaven on behalf of the earth; we stand in that role as priests, as reconcilers. God really wants to use us to transform our cities and communities.

In previous chapters, we have discussed the joy and privilege we have to love our city through Jesus, as well as the responsibility to defend the people in our cities from the destructive work of the enemy. That is an awesome responsibility that we must take seriously. If only we understood better the authority and power God grants to us in the place of prayer! When we realize that we can impact the rates of suicide, murder, divorce, and other devastating consequences of our captivity, we will hopefully rise up and take our places as watchmen and gatekeepers.

What hope does your city have if there is no functioning priesthood? Think of the broken lives in your city—those torn by divorce, suicide, drugs, crime, immorality, murder of innocent and defenseless little lives through abortion, sexual and physical abuse, neglect of the poor and disadvantaged, and so on. Brokenness is seen everywhere in our cities.

> JESUS WILL RELEASE JUSTICE ON EARTH IN RESPONSE TO NIGHT AND DAY INTERCESSION.

Through intercession, we can bring people in our city before the throne of God, defending them against the enemy, who the Bible says is the "accuser of the brethren." People are being accused day and night; their lives are being ravaged by the enemy. What hope do people have if there is no one mediating on their behalf in the throne room of heaven? They have no hope for justice! There is a righteous Judge on the throne, and He hears the cry of the intercessor mediating on behalf of the people in their cities.

Many people pray when they need divine intervention, but if they don't know Jesus or know somebody that can intercede on their behalf, they have no hope that their prayers are being heard, let alone answered. They hope someone is up there who can help them, so they call on an unknown force. But they don't know His love; they don't know He hears them and longs for fellowship with them.

There is a promise in Luke 18. Jesus says,

> And shall God not avenge His own elect who cry out day and night to Him, though He bears long with them? I tell you that He will avenge them speedily. Nevertheless, when the Son of Man comes, will He find faith on the earth? (Luke 18:7–8)

Jesus will release justice on earth in response to night and day intercession. We stand before the Lord night and day to cry out for justice, and the Bible promises that God will release it.

## ESTABLISHING A CANOPY OF PRAYER

As the corporate church begins to intercede on behalf of its city, a grace "canopy" made possible by prayer begins to cover the city. That means it is possible for the church in a local region to begin to pray in agreement for the purposes of God to come down to earth. Jesus promises us, "If two of you agree on earth concerning anything that they ask, it will be done for them by My Father who is in heaven" (Matt. 18:19). When that kind of agreement happens, heaven begins to touch and influence the earth!

The goal is for His kingdom to come and His will to be done as it already exists in heaven. Do you realize God already has a will for your city? It is already in His heart. The question is, who is going to pray for His will to become a reality on earth?

> And the fire on the altar shall be kept burning on it; it shall not be put out. And the priest shall burn wood on it every morning,

and lay the burnt offering in order on it; and he shall burn on it the fat of the peace offerings. A fire shall always be burning on the altar; it shall never go out. (Leviticus 6:12–13)

The most critical component of transformation is sustained, fervent intercession. James clearly says, "The effective, fervent prayer of a righteous man avails much" (5:15). This is often a missing element in our ministry efforts. We pray for half an hour and then go out and try to change the city! When Jesus gave instruction to His disciples, He told them to "wait" *until* the promise of the Father, the power of the Holy Spirit, was given to them. He didn't say to pray for one hour and then go out and do something. We must wait *until* we are endued with power! The fruit we have in our ministry will be directly proportional to the amount of prayer we engage in.

While it is important to plan and strategize for our ministry activities, we must keep such planning in the right order of priorities. Our first priority must be to see God's presence restored; then we must pray until we hear His voice and understand what the "Spirit says to the churches" (Rev. 3:6). Only then can we be obedient to follow His instructions and work out a plan of response.

Our ministry endeavors should be only *in response* to what we have heard from the Lord! If our ministry activities don't originate in the throne room with God's direction, why do we expect Him to validate them with His presence and power?

A. W. Tozer made the comment, "There is little that we need other than God himself. The evil practice of seeking God *and . . .* effectively prevents us from finding God in full revelation." He continues, "If we omit the *and* we shall soon find God, and in Him we shall find that for which we have all our lives been secretly longing."[1]

## REMNANT PRINCIPLE

There is a hope-filled principle in the Bible—God rarely uses a majority to accomplish His purposes! God uses a minority of people, a faithful remnant, who are faithfully obedient to His Word. A good example of the remnant principle in the Bible is the story of Gideon. Israel was being so terrorized by the Midianites that they were living in caves in the mountains. In Judges 6, it says that the Lord had given them over to the enemy because Israel "did evil in the eyes of the

Lord" (v. 1). So for seven years the Lord allowed the Midianites to invade and ravage the land of Israel, until the people "cried out to the Lord for help" (v. 6). In response, the Lord chose a man named Gideon to deliver Israel from their troubles.

THERE IS A HOPE-FILLED PRINCIPLE IN THE BIBLE—GOD RARELY USES A MAJORITY TO ACCOMPLISH HIS PURPOSES!

Gideon was quite surprised to find himself in this situation and questioned the Lord, saying, "But Lord, how can I save Israel? My clan is the weakest in Manasseh, and I am the least in my family" (v. 15 NIV). The Lord simply responded, "I will be with you, and you will strike down the Midianites as if they were but one man" (v. 16 NIV). Apparently Gideon's weakness and humility qualified him rather than disqualified him!

In response to God, Gideon assembled a small army of about thirty-two thousand men. But the Lord told him, "You have too many men for me to deliver Midian into their hands. In order that Israel may not boast against me that her own strength has saved her" (Judg. 7:2 NIV). God instructed Gideon two times to sift out the men. The first sifting caused twenty-two thousand to turn back, and the second sifting left Gideon with only three hundred men! This was a mere 1 percent of the original troops. By following the clear instruction that the Lord gave Gideon this small number routed the enemy easily, just as God had promised.

This is an important principle: God wants to make it clear that it is He and not our own wisdom or strength that defeats the enemy. Sometimes He has to sift us—our resources and finances—to make the situation so totally impossible that, when the breakthrough comes, He is the only one who receives the glory. The good news is that God plus us, in all of our frailty and weakness, equals the majority God needs to accomplish His purposes!

Throughout church history and in current testimonies of transformation, we see God's fire originating and then spreading from a handful of faithful, praying, persevering saints. Changing a city doesn't require a crowd but it does require believers who are living lives of radical obedience to Jesus.

## LIVING SACRIFICES

When we are hungry and desperate for God's presence to be restored in tangible ways in our lives, the church, and our communities, we will become obedient to the task of intercession. Because we have lost our desperation, the living sacrifices have crawled off the altar! The altars are empty, and yet we are standing on the sidelines pleading with God to send revival. I believe God is waiting for us—the living sacrifices—to get back on the altars of prayer. Otherwise, what is He to consume with His fire? We cannot disconnect ourselves from this process. God doesn't send revival as a concept, a method, or an activity that is disconnected from His body. We are the living sacrifices He consumes with His fiery presence!

> I beseech you therefore, brethren, by the mercies of God, that you present your bodies a living sacrifice, holy, acceptable to God, which is your reasonable service. (Romans 12:1)

Human strategies don't bring revival; revival comes when God sends fire on living sacrifices. Fire from God's throne doesn't fall without sacrifices; neither does fire fall on empty altars. God waits to send His fire until the sacrifice is prepared and laid on the altar. This is what touches the heart of God! He is waiting for us to be laid before Him as living sacrifices, and then He comes and consumes us as incense that becomes a precious aroma before Him in heaven.

> "Even them I will bring to My holy mountain, and make them joyful in My house of prayer. Their burnt offerings and their sacrifices will be accepted on My altar; for My house shall be called a house of prayer for all nations" (Isaiah 56:7).

Not only are we consumed by God's presence when we are willing to be living sacrifices, but we can also connect God's presence to the people living in our communities. There is a picture in the Old Testament of David bringing the ark of the covenant, which contained God's presence, to Jerusalem. The ark was carried on the shoulders of the priests. That's the same thing God wants us to do today; the priests in the city should be ushering in the presence of God.

When the corporate church of a city rebuilds the altars of prayer and worships and prays together, the city becomes an altar of sacrifice and the aroma rises before the Lord.

We see this illustrated in 2 Chronicles when Solomon dedicated the temple to the Lord. When Solomon had completed the preparation of the sacrifice and the altar, God's fire came and consumed the sacrifice and His glory filled the temple. All of Israel fell down and worshiped. Then God says this: "I have heard your prayer, and have chosen this place for Myself as a house of sacrifice" (2 Chron. 7:12).

He continues: "Now My eyes will be open and My ears attentive to prayer made in this place. For now I have chosen and sanctified this house, that My name may be there forever; and My eyes and My heart will be there perpetually" (2 Chron. 7:15–16). One of the first steps in the journey toward transformation is simply to get God's attention. We want Him to turn His face back toward our community!

Our motivation in gaining God's attention is not so He can come and do things for us—He is not a spiritual handyman for our lists and agendas. Our motivation must come out of a holy desperation for His presence—we cannot live another day without His presence in our midst! Oh that we would recognize our desperate need for His presence!

## BECOMING A CORPORATE "ESTHER"

Esther was an orphan girl who through sovereign selection and much preparation won the heart of the king of Persia and became the queen. God used Esther and her relationship with the king to save the Jewish people from annihilation by the enemy. Esther had favor with the king because she was the object of his affection.

This is how the corporate church should be approaching the Lord on behalf of the people in our cities. We must approach our King based upon our identity as His beloved. This role of bridal intercession with King Jesus is a place of identifying with the people who are targeted by the enemy for destruction; it's a place of intimacy and incredible spiritual authority.

As we come before the Lord in prayer and worship, His heart is moved by our love and devotion. He extends His favor and authority to us and sentences of destruction written over the lives of the people in our communities are defeated!

A day is coming when large gatherings of worshiping intercessors will be contending for God's presence to be restored and for strongholds in the city to be uprooted. The unified church will be the answer to the prayer of Jesus in John 17:21, "that they all may be one, as You, Father, are in Me, and I in You; that they also may be one in Us that the world may believe that You have sent Me." In that moment God will lead us into such effective prayer that the "death sentences" written for the people in our cities will be overturned. And because of His love for His bride, God's heart will be moved to respond to us. Jesus will answer our desperate intercession on behalf of our cities!

We must abandon ourselves to pursue God's heart when crying out for justice to come to our cities. Then, confident of the love of the King, we can pour out our hearts before Him in expectation. Assured of His love toward us, we can declare as Esther did in the face of the enemy: "If I perish, I perish!"

*You have been called into the kingdom for such a time as this!*

# Chapter 11

# BUILDING THE
# HOUSE OF THE LORD

"HEAVEN IS MY THRONE, AND EARTH IS MY
FOOTSTOOL. WHERE IS THE HOUSE THAT YOU
WILL BUILD FOR ME? AND WHERE IS
THE PLACE OF MY REST?"

ISAIAH 66:1

Have you ever wondered what draws the Lord's presence to a city? Can we welcome the presence of God to our community? If we want the Lord Jesus to inhabit our communities, we must build Him a dwelling place where His presence can come and rest among us.

How do we build a dwelling place for God? And for what purpose do we build it? Obviously, it's not something God needs, nor can He be contained within it. God is not looking for a structure made by human hands; He is looking for a dwelling place both in our hearts individually and also in His body corporately. What is God looking for? "But on this one I will look: on him who is poor and of a contrite spirit, and who trembles at My word" (Isa. 66:2). The Lord is longing to draw near and dwell with those who are humble and contrite, those who tremble before Him. God is longing for a place to "rest" in us and in our cities. Paul talks about this building principle in Ephesians 2:

You are no longer strangers and foreigners, but fellow citizens with the saints and of the household of God, having been built on the foundation of the apostles and prophets, Jesus Christ Himself being the chief cornerstone, in whom the whole building, being joined together, grows into a holy temple in the Lord, in whom you also are being built together for a habitation of God in the Spirit. (19–22)

The dwelling place that God is building must rest on the cornerstone of Jesus Christ. In Psalm 118:22, it says, "The stone which the builders rejected has become the chief cornerstone." We must build everything we do on Jesus as the cornerstone of the foundation. Then, on that foundation, we are joined together and become a "holy temple in the Lord," a dwelling place of God in the Spirit.

Why would the Lord instruct us to build a dwelling place for His Spirit if He didn't intend to come and dwell in it? Jesus prays for this very thing in John 17:

"I do not pray for these alone, but also for those who will believe in Me through their word; that they all may be one, as You, Father, are in Me, and I in You; that they also may be one in Us, that the world may believe that You have sent Me. And the glory which You gave Me I have given them, that they may be one just as We are one: I in them, and You in Me; that they may be made perfect in one, and that the world may know that You have sent Me, and have loved them as You have loved Me" (20–23).

When the church is dwelling together in unity, the world will see and recognize Jesus in His church! The harvest that is coming won't be a result of our clever methods; it will come as we, His body, reflect the nature and aroma of Jesus himself.

## GOD'S DWELLING PLACE

The Lord is doing a new thing in the hearts of His people, drawing us and building us together so that His presence can dwell among us in tangible ways.

The house God is building is not a material structure; it is not determined by church tradition or denominational affiliation, particular theology or ethnicity. He is building a new covenant house, where His blood-washed people *are* His temple. The house God is building is simply a unified, praying church. Jesus said, "Is it not written, 'My house shall be called a house of prayer for all nations'?" (Mark 11:17). Prayer lies at the very heart of what God is doing and building.

Every local congregation is important to the Lord and represents an important part of the full expression of Him in the city. But the true sense of the house of the Lord is larger than the local congregations. The house of the Lord is the corporate expression of Christ's church in a city or geographic region. Although individual congregations continue to express themselves according to their particular vision and values, there is a broader corporate context for the church in any city or area.

In 1 Corinthians, chapter 3, Paul emphasizes that the foundation for God's building is Jesus Christ and we are fellow workers who build on that foundation together. The most critical component we build in ministry is the foundation—is it being established on the right foundation? Is the foundation strong enough to support the structure being built on it? Are we building with "fellow workers"?

Often people will try to build "skyscrapers" of vision on two inches of spiritual foundation, but it doesn't work! Scripture illustrates the wisdom of building a house on a rock versus sand, to point out that one will last and the other will not survive the storms that come. The same is true for our ministries, especially when we partner with the body of Christ in our communities. Our foundation in Jesus must be firmly established along with our relational foundation with one another.

Christ's church in the city will emerge when there is mutual affection and concern expressed among the congregations, when they honor one another and submit to one another regarding their city.

## WHAT ARE WE BUILDING?

Do you ever wonder what is really being accomplished through all our ministry activities? One of the deceptions in the Western church is that if we are busy, we assume we are building *something*. Surely with all the communication, promotion, conferences, books, teaching tapes, and newsletters we must be building the kingdom, we think. Not necessarily! Psalm 127:1 reminds us: "Unless the Lord builds the house, they labor in vain who build it; unless the Lord guards the city, the watchman stays awake in vain." It is possible, even very likely, that our busyness *is not* an indicator of how fruitful we really are. Sometimes busyness becomes rhetoric that disguises itself as productive ministry. Are we going to live in rhetoric or reality?

In the book of Haggai, the Lord is referring to the same problem with the people living in Jerusalem. He says to His prophet, "This people say: 'the time has not come, the time that the Lord's house should be built'" (1:2). The people made their own decision not to build God's house, continuing to build nice houses for themselves instead.

The Lord goes on to ask them a very important question: "Is it time for you yourselves to dwell in your paneled houses, and this temple to lie in ruins?" (Hag. 1:4). I believe the Lord is asking His church the same question right now, "Is it time for us to build our own individual lives and ministries while the house of the Lord lies in ruins?"

> ARE WE GOING TO LIVE IN RHETORIC OR REALITY?

The Lord continues:

> Consider your ways! You have sown much, and bring in little; you eat, but do not have enough; you drink, but you are not filled with drink; you clothe yourselves, but no one is warm; and he who earns wages, earns wages to put into a bag with holes. . . . You looked for much, but indeed it came to little; and when you brought it home, I blew it away. (Haggai 1:5–6, 9a)

Does that sound familiar? Have you ever wondered why all our labor in ministry doesn't provide the results we hope for? This Scripture provides the answer. "Why?" says the LORD of hosts. "Because of My house that is in ruins, while every one of you runs to his own house" (Hag. 1:9b).

Basically, God says that the decision the people made to build their own houses hadn't produced any fruit. We have been very busy in the Western church, but what have we been building of significance? Is it "coming to little"? And the Lord tells them that the little fruit they *did* produce He blew away—He didn't want it.

We invite His presence into the houses that we are building as if we want Him to come and rearrange the furniture! The truth is, Jesus isn't going to add His glory to our fleshly efforts and He cannot possibly fit inside our dwelling. He isn't coming for a remodeling project—He is coming as a conquering King to establish His kingdom.

God presents a solution to this situation: "Thus says the LORD of hosts: 'Consider your ways! Go up to the mountains and bring wood and build the temple, that I may take pleasure in it and be glorified'" (Hag. 1:7–8).

We must consider our ways! We must build His temple and worship Him together so that He is glorified! Our refusal to build God's house has had a serious impact on our communities. The Lord continues in Haggai:

> Therefore the heavens above you withhold the dew, and the earth withholds its fruit. For I called for a drought on the land and the mountains, on the grain and the new wine and the oil, on whatever the ground brings forth, on men and livestock, and on all the labor of your hands. (1:10–11)

## THE HOUSE OF THE LORD

The Lord is building His house not only for His benefit but also for our own. He knows the days ahead of us; He knows what is coming. He knows we cannot sustain life if we are only building our own individual houses. There must be a house built among His people so that He can come and dwell among us. In Haggai, the Lord encourages Zerubbabel by saying,

> My Spirit remains among you; do not fear! For thus says the LORD of hosts: "Once more (it is a little while) I will shake heaven and earth, the sea and the dry land; and I will shake all nations, and they shall come to the Desire of All Nations, and I will fill this temple with glory," says the LORD of hosts. "The silver is Mine, and the gold is Mine," says the LORD of hosts. "The glory of this latter temple shall be greater than the former," says the LORD of hosts. "And in this place I will give peace" (2:4–9).

God has a plan to restore His glory to His house! The glory coming will be preceded by a great shaking in the earth that will cause many to turn toward Jesus—the Desire of the Nations. In that day, the house of the Lord will be established on the earth; it will be a place of refuge, purity, and glory.

David shares the depth of his longing to build God's house in Psalm 69: "Zeal for Your house has eaten me up" (Ps. 69:9). We must become zealous to build the house of the Lord! David further states his determination to find a dwelling place for God in Psalm 132:

> Surely I will not go into the chamber of my house, or go up to the comfort of my bed; I will not give sleep to my eyes or slumber to my eyelids, until I find a place for the Lord, a dwelling place for the Mighty One of Jacob. (3–5)

Are we consumed with zeal for the house of the Lord? Or are we resting comfortably even though the house of the Lord is lying in ruins?

## LIVING STONES

When God builds a house, what does He use for building material? *We* are the living stones that God uses to build His house:

> Coming to Him as to a living stone, rejected indeed by men, but chosen by God and precious, *you also, as living stones, are being built up a spiritual house,* a holy priesthood, to offer up spiritual sacrifices acceptable to God through Jesus Christ. (1 Peter 2:4, emphasis added)
>
> In whom the whole building, being joined together, grows into a holy temple in the Lord, in whom *you also are being built together for a habitation of God* in the Spirit. (Ephesians 2:21–22, emphasis added)

As living stones we must be broken and purified before we can reflect His glory. There is a process of brokenness and preparation involved before the living stone can be "fit" into the wall of a house. The Lord wants to take us from "opaqueness" to "translucence" so we reflect His beauty, fragrance, and glory. Something that is opaque absorbs light, while translucent or transparent objects allow light to pass through them and be reflected. When we are full of darkness we can't help but be absorbing and self-focused. Pain does that to a person. But when we have been broken and purified we become reflectors of His light and life, carriers of His glory. We, then, as the Lord's body will reflect Him to the world around us.

There is an interesting question in the book of Nehemiah, asked by the enemy who was desperately trying to stop the people of God from rebuilding the walls of the city: "What are these people doing? Are they going to rebuild the walls with *burned* stones?" (4:2, emphasis added). The enemy was trying to intimidate the people by pointing out the weakness and brokenness of the material they were using to rebuild the city. What they didn't realize is that in God's economy weakness and brokenness are qualifiers for His grace and strength! So their answer to the question is yes! That is *exactly* what God did and longs to do—take burned stones and turn them into living stones that He will use to rebuild the city.

## JESUS LONGS TO GATHER US!

When Jesus approached Jerusalem before His death, we see Him weeping over the city, saying, "How often I have longed to gather your children together, as a hen gathers her chicks under her wings, but you were not willing!" He then goes on to prophesy the destruction of the city saying, "Look, your house is left to you desolate. I tell you, you will not see me again until you say, 'Blessed is he who comes in the name of the Lord'" (Luke 13:34–35 NIV). Then in Luke 19:44, He says that this destruction comes to Jerusalem because "you did not know the time of your visitation." They missed the hour of their visitation. How? Well, they were looking for something different. They were inside the temple studying about the Messiah even as Jesus was walking around Jerusalem doing all kinds of signs and miracles. The Pharisees inside the temple were reading about the coming Messiah, and they missed the fulfillment right before their eyes in the person of Jesus.

Jesus is building himself a house. He is gathering the living stones and fitting us together to become His dwelling place. As we begin to worship, pray, and minister together with common vision and purpose, the wall of protection around our city rises.

When we enter into covenant with God and with one another on behalf of our community, we will then be given our "building permits" from the Lord to build His house. "The earth is the Lord's, and the fullness thereof" (Ps. 24:1 KJV), but we must still walk in that authority, commit to the land where we dwell, and obtain the permit to build God's house there. In the natural world you can't build a house on property you don't own or have authority over. The same is true in the spiritual. If we haven't accepted God's invitation to covenant with the land we live in, we don't have His authority to build on it.

## DIVINE PARTNERSHIP EQUALS DIVINE FRUITFULNESS!

We have become the temple of the Lord and the dwelling place of God individually. There is a personal dimension to having Him dwell in our hearts, but there is also a corporate expression of having Him dwell in a city through His body.

An awesome testimony of what happens when the body of Christ decides to build together to attract the presence of the Lord is a recent partnership between the International House of Prayer and the Promise Keepers organization.

The International House of Prayer is a ministry of nonstop worship with prayer that began in May 1999 and has since September 1999 continued twenty-four hours a day, 365 days a year. It's basically one continuous prayer meeting! The House of Prayer is led by Mike Bickle and is staffed by almost five hundred people who are ministering to the Lord night and day through prayer, worship, and fasting. In addition, they are being equipped to fulfill the Great Commission by reaching out in evangelism, prophetic ministry, healing the sick, and feeding the poor.

Promise Keepers is an organization dedicated to ministering the reality of Jesus Christ to millions of men across our nation. Through stadium and arena conferences, radio programming, multimedia resources, and outreach to local churches, Promise Keepers encourages men to live godly lives and to keep seven basic promises of commitment to God, their families, and others in the context of the local church. Promise Keepers was founded by Coach Bill McCartney and marked its tenth anniversary in the year 2000, having reached more than 3.5 million men through ninety-eight stadium and arena conferences.[1]

At the International House of Prayer we are contending 24/7 for the fullness of God's presence to come to our city! So when Promise

Keeper leaders invited us to partner with them in their event in Kansas City we wholeheartedly agreed. As we met together and sought the Lord about how we could unite in this effort, we realized the Lord had something very special in mind. Each organization laid down its own agendas and structures and acknowledged that the Lord was building something new in our midst. We wanted that! While it wasn't easy bridging two ministries together, we all agreed that God's purpose was our highest goal and so we continued to submit to that. We were amazed how the Lord "built" us together for His purposes.

The International House of Prayer moved down to the Kemper Arena with hundreds of intercessors and worship teams to serve the Promise Keepers event through continuous prayer and worship.

The night before the conference started, we brought children down to the arena and together we prayed over each seat! It was an amazing sight to see those kids, some as young as six years old, earnestly praying for the men who would sit in the seats. Some of them had been praying for specific seat numbers, believing God would touch that father or brother as he attended the meeting. I asked one little boy what he was praying for and he said, "that this man's hard heart, which is like a rock, would melt." As we began to pray through the empty arena, the presence of the Lord began to fill the place. It felt like a heavy fog rolling in. Soon the once-empty arena was turned into a sanctuary!

We started the "prayer furnace" at twelve noon the next day and continued for thirty hours of nonstop prayer and worship. The intercession was intense for the duration. The presence of the Lord and the power at work contending for the men in that arena were incredible!

That evening an altar call for salvation was planned, and we arranged for a live video feed TV monitor in the prayer room. We were able to watch the altar call response even as we prayed for the men in the arena, watching the fruit of our intercession in "real time." We prayed earnestly for the men to commit their lives to Jesus, and then we watched as the men poured out onto the arena floor, crying out to the Lord. More than four thousand decision cards were handed out, but the aisles on the second level were so jammed, nobody could even get up there to them!

A touch of revival occurred in the arena that weekend. There were five *spontaneous* altar calls. Men were jumping over the railings trying to get to the front. There was a sweetness and presence of the Lord that many said they have never experienced before. The speakers were full of fire. The worship was anointed and continued longer that usual. Men were not only saved, some were also physically healed and delivered; thousands of men recommitted their lives and families back to Jesus.

One Promise Keeper leader referred to this event as "historic" because of the response to the altar call. He attributed the fruit to the partnership with worship and intercession that took place. Those of us in the International House of Prayer felt honored to participate in prayer for the harvest of souls. What a joy it was to serve the Lord together; Promise Keepers did their part, we did our part, and God (most important) did His part! It's a principle of Scripture that some plant, some water, but God gives the increase (1 Corinthians 3:6–7).

## GOD'S AGENDA VERSUS MAN'S AGENDA

Building the house of the Lord will require that we lay down some of our own agendas to seek how we can begin to build *together* according to God's purposes. We must discover how to build the house of the Lord with others—how we fit and how we can serve one another so that the message can be communicated in a much broader context.

We all have a basic instinct to hold on to our own agendas and try to maintain a sense of control. If we let go of it, we fear we'll lose everything. But it's a false fear. The truth is, in losing ourselves, we gain Jesus and His kingdom, but in trying to save ourselves, we gain nothing but self-centeredness. Matthew 6:33 says, "Seek first the kingdom of God and His righteousness, and all these things will be added to you." This is true on an individual level and on a corporate level.

While there are many unity efforts happening in cities, very few of them are dependent upon hearing the Lord together regarding His plans for the city. We can connect in heart and purpose only when that connection is first directed to heaven.

Jesus presented the kingdom of God as the total answer and promised that if we sought it first, then everything else would be added to us (Matthew 6:33). That is *really* true! We never lose when we seek God's kingdom purposes. Psalm 127:1 exhorts us: "Unless the LORD builds the house, they labor in vain who build it."

## BUILDING TOGETHER REQUIRES HUMILITY

If there is a "glue" that will hold us together in the building process, it's humility. It's an essential ingredient in the kingdom-building process.

Paul speaks of this in Ephesians 3 when he says,

> Walk worthy of the calling with which you were called, with all lowliness and gentleness, with longsuffering, bearing with one another in love, endeavoring to keep the unity of the Spirit in the bond of peace. (1–3)

The way to "walk worthy" of our calling is to do everything with lowliness or humility. Jesus came to us that way. He said about himself, "I am gentle and lowly in heart" (Matt. 11:29). He is our role model for how to walk out our callings. Paul goes on to say in Ephesians 4 that we need gentleness. Humble people tend to be gentle people because they aren't demanding, self-promoting, or harsh. Gentleness or meekness doesn't mean *weakness*! It means "strength under control." Finally, Paul says we need to be long-suffering, bearing with one another in love. That is a huge challenge. It means that when things don't go right or when we get offended or wounded by a brother, we don't have the option of walking away. To bear with one another, means to put up with someone with tenacious patience, choosing to love that one in his or her weakness, even as God loves us in ours.

These are not special requirements for the most spiritually mature believers. These are basic Christian character issues. Walking out our faith according to principles is *how* we become mature.

God is much more concerned about the maturity and character of His church than about our elaborate plans and programs. We know from James that "God resists the proud, but gives grace to the humble" (4:6), so our first order of business should be to get on God's side of that equation! We don't have a chance if God himself is opposing our ministry efforts and frustrating our plans. But if we take on the nature of Jesus and mature to the "fullness of Christ," then

God can work through us in ever-increasing effectiveness.

Humility is like oil that softens all the connecting points in the body of Christ. It allows rough spots to become smooth and allows grace to flow. It allows the character of Jesus to be formed in us. Humility causes us to be teachable, not arrogant, so we can learn to work together across various dividing lines, honoring and preferring one another.

When God doesn't oppose us but is drawn near, His presence gives reality to our unity. Psalm 133 promises a "commanded blessing" when we dwell together in unity. The blessing is His presence. It's all about Jesus.

## PREPARING A NEW WINESKIN FOR THE HARVEST

Jesus made it very clear that His house would be a house of prayer for all nations. There is an exciting collaboration beginning to take place on the earth between the prayer movement and mission organizations. The Lord wants us to connect the "vertical" dimension of prayer ministry before God's throne to the "horizontal" dimension of ministry to people.

God is building a global "net" of the connected, unified family of God joining together to complete the Great Commission. The net is being formed to prepare for the great harvest the Lord will release on the earth.

When God begins to "pour out His Spirit upon all flesh," as Joel promises (2:28), a harvest of souls will begin, and we must be prepared. The net must be strong, not loosely woven together; the intersections of relationships must be knotted and secure. This isn't about our own programs; it's about God's purposes to bring His gospel to the nations.

We need to prepare *now* for what God is sending *soon*. We must be people like Noah, who was willing to spend years building a boat (something nobody had ever seen or heard of) to prepare for a flood (that no one had ever seen or heard of). The ark that Noah built served as a container to rescue a remnant of humanity and living creatures, carrying them safely into a new season. When it begins to rain, it's too late to build the ark!

We must be determined to make a difference and contribute to building God's kingdom. If we are going to lead lives of significance and purpose, we must commit to living in a way that contributes to a building project that is larger than our own lives and will continue after we are gone—it's the kingdom of God!

Chapter 12

# TRANSFORMING VISION

"BEHOLD, I SAY TO YOU, LIFT UP YOUR EYES
AND LOOK AT THE FIELDS, FOR THEY ARE
ALREADY WHITE FOR HARVEST!"

JOHN 4:35

The first two sections of this book (calling the church back to her first love and out of her compromised condition) can be summed up in one word—*revival!* Once the church is revived and returns to her spiritual identity and role as an agent of change God can pour her out into the community to bring about life and healing. God's method of preparing His people is through revival in His church. The restoration of God's presence among His people is the cure for our complacency, boredom, double-mindedness, shallow methodologies, and superficial relationships.

Every true revival and city transformation effort begins in the heart of God. He initiates it; the intention begins with Him and is born of the Spirit through intercession and a humble seeking of Him as taught in 2 Chronicles 7:14. The promises of God and His redemptive purposes are stronger than the current state of captivity and disrepair in our cities.

## RESTORED VISION!

An important step in city transformation is to begin to see ourselves and our communities the way God sees us. We certainly need to see the reality of our condition, but we also need to have hope that God will bring restoration through His people. Most of what we hear on a daily basis are negative reports that focus on all the consequences of sin, lawlessness, and demonic activity in our communities (murders, rape, corruption, addictions). They receive free press to advertise their destructive activity! Everyone that Satan has successfully ruined or devastated in the last twenty-four hours shows up in your news media. That has tainted us. Our hearts have gotten sick and discouraged so we have given up on our cities; to us, they seem to be places that are impossible to fix. Our hearts have become either fearful or fascinated with the enemy's activities. Beloved, we need to get new eyes; we have to see our city from the Lord's perspective!

As the body of Christ is restored to intimacy and conformed to the image of Christ, the dullness is removed from our spiritual senses. Our ears, now attuned to the voice of our Bridegroom, are unplugged! Our eyes, turning away from distraction and seeking the face of Jesus, are opened! Our hearts, free from idolatry and compromise, begin to burn within us for His presence!

When Jesus said to His disciples in John 4:35, "Behold, I say to you, lift up your eyes and look at the fields, for they are already white for harvest," He didn't mean that in the natural sense, He meant it in the spiritual sense. He was referring to the harvest of souls that were ripe around them that Jesus could "see." He was encouraging them to see with spiritual eyes!

## COUNSEL OF JESUS

How do we move out of our place of compromise and complacency and back to the relevancy of the church seen in the book of Acts? Jesus gives us some important counsel in the third chapter of Revelation. This letter was written to a compromised church, not to unbelievers. He wrote this letter to the believers in Laodicea to encourage them to leave their compromise and prepare to be overcomers who share the authority and power of His throne.

First, He gives them a reality check on their condition:

> "I know your works, that you are neither cold nor hot. I wish you were cold or hot. So then, because you are lukewarm, and neither cold nor hot, I will spew you out of My mouth. Because you

say: I am rich, have become wealthy, and have need of nothing—and do not know that you are wretched, miserable, poor, blind, and naked" (Revelation 3:15–17).

Then He offers the following counsel:

> "I counsel you to buy from Me gold refined in the fire, that you may be rich; and white garments that you may be clothed, that the shame of your nakedness not be revealed; and anoint your eyes with eye salve, that you may see" (Revelation 3:18).

The only way to become spiritually "rich" is to be tested in the fire. Jesus encourages the Laodiceans to be refined so their impurities will be burned away and the valuable gold will remain. Then He encourages them to exchange their nakedness for pure garments of holiness, which He gives us to cover our shame. Finally, Jesus offers them eye salve to restore their spiritual eyesight. We must ask Jesus for eye salve so that our spiritual vision will be restored!

After His counsel to be delivered from their complacent condition, the Lord invites them to sit with Him on His throne: "To him who overcomes I will grant to sit with Me on My throne, as I also overcame and sat down with My Father on His throne" (Rev. 3:21). The exalted Lord Jesus is inviting us up to a higher reality, where He is sitting, to see what He is seeing!

After that invitation, John looks and sees "a door standing open in heaven" and a voice like a "trumpet" inviting him to "Come up here, and I will show you things which must take place after this" (Rev. 4:1).

## COME UP HIGHER!

In the same way He opened a door in heaven to show John the revelation, God longs to open doors of spiritual reality to us. He wants us to sit with Him in heavenly places. We must live with a spiritual vantage point from the throne room of God. The throne of God is the seat of His authority; it represents the place from which He rules and reigns over the nations. Jesus invites us to this place of authority and victory.

We have to see the Lord! We have to accept the invitation to come up higher around the throne, to behold Jesus, to see Him and believe! Once you see this, you have hope; and once we see what God sees, then we can come into agreement with His purposes. If we cannot see God's kingdom purposes, we cannot agree with them!

Revival is God's way of restoring His idea of normalcy. But we can't see what God sees with natural eyes; we need God-sized vision for God-sized purposes! When God is welcomed into a community and brings salvation, healing, and restoration, it will result in evidence of His intervention.

> IF WE CANNOT SEE GOD'S KINGDOM PURPOSES, WE CANNOT AGREE WITH THEM!

Take, for example, what God is doing in the nation of Fiji. The Sentinel Group released an exciting video entitled *Let the Seas Resound*.[1] This video documents a powerful transforming revival sweeping the nation of Fiji, which has led to the transformation of dozens of communities. Prompted by a military coup that sent the nation spiraling into violence and turmoil, the pastors unified and accepted responsibility for what they believed to be a consequence of their disunity. Joining together across denominational lines, they began to earnestly cry out to God for forgiveness and mercy. A once-fragmented body of Christ became a strong, unified voice raised to heaven in desperation. That cry was heard all through the land as tribal leaders began calling their villages to prayer meetings across the lawns of the village, humbling themselves before God, and pleading with God to send His presence to dwell among them.

Change began to happen quickly! Just thirty days before the national election, a new political party was formed, and by God's intervention a godly prime minister was elected. He, along with a God-fearing president, began to carefully place deeply committed Christians in top government positions. A former pastor became the president of the Senate, another former pastor now heads up the newly created National Ministry of Reconciliation. These leaders have led the way in calling the church to repentance and rededicating the nation to God.

A harvest of souls has begun; churches are filling with new converts. Some of the new believers include the military leaders who staged the coup in 2000! They were led to the Lord in prison. In one jail, where some of the leaders are held, sounds of worship can be heard outside the prison walls. Hearing the roar of worship coming from inside, some people confuse it with a church. Can you imagine that?

God is touching the nation of Fiji and responding to the cry of the people. One of the most noted features of the revival in Fiji is the pervasive influence the revival is having through so many spheres of society. Transformation is happening in the church, in politics, in the economy, in ecology, and in business. Many signs and wonders are also occurring in nature. Coral reefs are being renewed almost overnight, following decades of disintegration; fish that had nearly disappeared for fifty years have returned in abundance. The fruit trees that were barren are now bending over with the weight of ripe, abundant fruit.

To us, these reports sound amazing and unusual. But how does God view them? What is God's idea of a healthy community? God's highest intention for the nation of Fiji isn't poverty, violence, rebellion, disunity, and barrenness. Once the church renewed its covenant with God, He could bring them into His covenant promises, giving them the land of their inheritance. I believe God is simply restoring life as He intended it, according to His divine goodness and purpose. The prosperity and fruitfulness of the land in these communities is actually God's idea of "normal." We have settled for so much less than God longs to give us!

What is it God longs to give to you and your community? Can you see it? Do you believe it? This would be a good place to pause and consider before the Lord: *What does He have in mind for me?*

## WHAT DO WE SEE?

We have become convinced by the enemy and our own unbelief that our communities are too difficult to change. It's impossible to look at our surroundings in the natural and have faith. If we want to be filled with fresh faith and vision, we have to *look up!* We need a glimpse of God's glory and a heavenly perspective. We need to ask the Lord to put our cities in His perspective and remove the spirit of unbelief from our hearts. We must see our city or community through eyes filled with His glory and purpose, trusting Him to bring those promises to pass.

In Hebrews 11:8, the writer describes Abraham as a man who lived by faith, not knowing where he was going but being led by the promise of God. Abraham was looking for a city "with foundations, whose architect and builder is God" (NIV). Abraham, like many heroes in Hebrews 11, was a person who had "seen" the promises of God in his spirit and had lived his life according to that reality without seeing the evidence of them in the natural.

That is very challenging! I have a difficult time waiting for a couple of weeks to see something fulfilled that I have prayed for! In our culture we are spoiled by how quickly we get whatever we want; we very rarely have to wait for anything. Even if we don't have the money to buy it outright, we are allowed to "borrow" and purchase things on paper for years, until the transaction is actually completed and all the money is fully paid back. This has created a false sense of obtaining what we want without waiting or sacrificing for it. This culture has affected us spiritually as well, causing us to trust in programs or promises of quick results. But the things of God aren't obtained quickly or without sacrifice. His economy is quite the opposite! His kingdom will cost us everything, and we aren't promised the reward of seeing it fulfilled before we die.

We have to renew our minds and hearts to begin seeing and thinking with an eternal perspective. The race we are running isn't a sprint—it's a marathon. It won't be completed in the next six months or two years, no matter how many books or television programs tell you differently. We have to settle in our hearts that what God has called us to is an eternal kingdom and what we get on this side is only a glimpse of reality.

## "CITY OF THE BRIDE"

A great testimony of a city that has gained a heavenly perspective and is preparing for long-term transformation is Guildford, England. The leaders of the city have been pursuing the transformation of their community primarily by focusing on establishing covenant with each other, realizing their identity and purpose as the bride of Christ to bring healing and restoration to their community. I have had the privilege of joining the city on their journey and have enjoyed watching what the Lord is doing among them. What began as a handful of people captured by God's heart and purposes, has now filtered through to the pastors and leaders of the city and into every arena of community life. This is an account of how the Lord is working to transform individuals, a company, and now a city into the "City of the Bride":

> Just over four years ago Julian Watts in Guildford (England) was a partner in a consultancy practice, working with multinational corporations around the world. In spiritual terms, he based his value in God by his ability to give finances to the church. In 1999 Julian said "yes" to the Lord's invitation to step out in faith to build a new Internet company called "Markets Unlocked." The business grew very quickly, riding on the crest of the Internet wave. But the "dot-com" crash that swiftly followed in the year 2000 was brutal, all but wiping the company out. As things were getting worse, the non-Christians in the company left and the remaining Christians started praying together—first monthly, then as things got worse, weekly, and finally—as desperation set in—daily!
>
> The more time they spent with the Lord, the more things began to change. Gradually the list of urgent prayer requests gave way to simply worshipping Jesus and the conference room soon became the company prayer room. The Corporate Communications Director, Liz Jones, no longer had much to communicate about and started spending more and more of her time in the prayer room, worshipping the Lord and praying for the company.
>
> The more they worshiped, the more the Lord began to intervene directly to sustain the business. Daily routines began to change, too, as prayer and personal time with Jesus became the priority of their workday. In addition to their personal prayer time, Tuesdays became a corporate prayer time from ten until noon. Everyone in the company would meet, along with local pastors and intercessors, to worship and pray.
>
> Liz Jones, in her new role, became a trailblazer for the rest of the company. During the hours she spent in the Lord's presence, the Lord started speaking to her about her personal identity as part of the bride of Christ. Increasingly, the Lord started speaking this message of intimacy to other people in the company as well. In the midst of all the difficult circumstances, Jesus was wooing them as His bride. Individually, they were starting to understand their personal identity as part of His bride, and they began to respond to

Him with an intimacy they had never experienced before.

By late 2001 the Lord had carried them through a painful wilderness season and in the process had completely transformed all the commercial aspects of the company—their business strategy, organizational structure, staff, operational processes, location, and everything else—from man's best designs to God's blueprint. The heart and driving force of the company became the presence of Jesus in their midst!

During their prayer times, the Lord had gradually drawn them into greater and greater intercession for their city, and He overwhelmed them with His love for Guildford. He gave them the passage from Isaiah 61:10–62:5 and told them to declare it, using the name of the city. As Guildford has one of the highest divorce rates in Europe, the names "Forsaken" and "The Deserted Wife" in the passage from Isaiah had immense impact, as did the new name the Lord was giving the city—"Happily Married."

At the same time the Lord was transforming the company, He was also beginning to connect them to pastors and leaders who were praying together in the city. At citywide meetings, the leaders began to declare God's promises from Isaiah over the city, calling Guildford into her true identity as a city of the bride. The pastors, leaders, and laypeople involved began to "see" their city as God intended, as a city of refuge, a city to release wealth to evangelize the nations, and a city filled with stable, healthy marriages and families.

As leaders gathered they envisioned each sphere of society as transformed through intimacy with Jesus. Their desire is to see every arena of the city—business, education, family, arts, and entertainment—transformed by God's love and power! They want God's kingdom to come to their city and for Guildford to be a "City of the Bride."[2]

## ETERNAL PERSPECTIVE

Like the leaders in Guildford, we must begin to understand our corporate identity as the bride of Christ and to see our communities through the eyes of the Lord. What is it He wants us to see? I believe it is His kingdom as it exists in heaven; He wants us to believe that the essential reality of His kingdom *can* come to earth. We must see His reality and look beyond the natural eye in order to do this. We are called to an eternal kingdom. We have to have eyes to see eternally in order that we may agree with His purposes for our families, communities, and cities.

What you see and then believe is what you will be willing to give your life to. That vision will determine the choices you make about simple but important things, like how you spend your time and your money. Ultimately, your vision will determine what you will live for and what you are willing to die for. Do you have a vision from the Lord that you are willing to pursue with your whole heart? Is it worth dying for? If not, you probably haven't connected with His vision and perspective about His purposes for your community.

Paul prays in Ephesians 1:17–19:

> . . . that the God of our Lord Jesus Christ, the Father of glory, may give to you the spirit of wisdom and revelation in the knowledge of Him, the eyes of your understanding being enlightened; that you may know what is the hope of His calling, what are the riches of the glory of His inheritance in the saints, and what is the exceeding greatness of His power toward us who believe, according to the working of His mighty power.

Without a vision, people are doomed to live mediocre lives, carried along by social influences and self-centered interests. The Bible says, "Where there is no vision, the people perish" (Prov. 29:18 KJV). Our own vision for our lives cannot sustain us; we must have a vision that originates from the heart of God, from His very throne room. His vision is life-giving, life-changing, and worth abandoning our hearts and lives to.

INTIMACY RESTORES SPIRITUAL VISIBILITY.

What is our vision full of? The more time we spend in fellowship with Jesus, the more He changes our perspective and allows us to see things from His vantage point. Intimacy restores spiritual visibility.

When we are clouded by our own ambition, unbelief, insecurities, and pride, we cannot hope to see from heaven's perspective. The church has so many filters on her eyes; her spiritual sight has grown dim. Many things have distracted and clouded our vision. We have become enamored with our own ideas and revelation, or that of another person. But if we want to be totally overwhelmed by revelation, creativity, and power, we must take a glance toward God's throne room!

When we are confronted with the incompatible realities of the natural versus the supernatural, we must choose which one to believe. Walking by faith requires that we choose the supernatural as the *higher* reality. We must know the mind of Jesus and then come into agreement with it. Our renewed mind leads to more discernment, because that *is* the reality! The enemy wants to use natural reality to obscure true reality. It's a choice we must make: Will we die to self to pursue true life in Jesus?

## IMPORTANT TRANSITIONS FOR KINGDOM VISION

God is preparing His body for mighty exploits! One of the ways He is preparing us is by challenging our current paradigms or mindsets so He can renew our minds. We cannot fulfill our purposes if we are living with a wrong mindset or with clouded vision. There are important transitions that have begun to happen in the church over the last several years. There are encouraging "shifts" in our thinking and our approach to ministry taking place. These shifts are helping us make the transition required to prepare both the church and the community for spiritual awakening and transformation. We must be "transformed by the renewing of our minds" (Rom. 12:2) and gain a kingdom perspective before we can prepare ourselves for transformation. Here are some key paradigm shifts that are beginning to occur:

### 1. From Suspicion to Trust

As expressions of citywide prayer have increased and gained momentum in the last several years, many Christians have moved from feeling suspicious of one another to trusting one another. We are realizing that not only is it possible to pray together for our city, but it is also very beneficial. There are benefits both to us personally and to the people of our city. Today we're not as likely to consider our denominational "labels" as the determining factor in whether or not we can trust one another. People are working together in cities all over the world, willing to share their ministries for the glory of God. This is a new season for the church, and the possibilities for what God has in mind for us to build together are exciting!

## 2. Functional Unity to Relational Unity

As our unity has grown, so has our desire to deepen our fellow-ship—to move from "event-based" unity to "relational" unity. Event-based unity is agreeing to be unified together for the sake of a ministry project. Then when the project is completed, we go back to business as usual. Many leaders are moving to a deeper level of relationship with one another and have experienced real covenant friendship. They aren't satisfied to just "do things" together. In the same vein, many have decided that they want to relate to Jesus in the same way. Rather than summoning His help for our projects, we want Jesus to manifest His presence among us—we want *Him*.

## 3. Horizontal Agreement to Vertical Agreement

Most of our ministry efforts have focused on our unity and agreement with one another, when the truth is that we need to be more concerned with our unity and agreement with the Lord. We gather in our meetings to listen to one another's ideas and agendas and to promote our own. But no matter how much we talk to one another, we will never have the wisdom of God. The wisdom of God is from heaven, and if we want it, we must seek the Lord together until He gives us His mind. Horizontal unity is important once we are in vertical agreement with God. Christians are growing weary of pursuing unity for unity's sake without a heavenly agenda and perspective.

## 4. Revival Visitation to Transforming Habitation

Now that we realize that God intends to transform our cities, and not just visit them, our prayer focus has shifted from the "visitation" of God to the lasting "habitation" of God. Of course we want God to visit, but now we really want Him to stay! Our focus is also shifting from seeking revival inside the church to the exciting impact of a revived church—the transformation of the community outside the church. When God pours out His Spirit and revives His church, and His people carry that revival fire out into their spheres of influence in the community, the lost come in contact with Jesus and the transformation of institutions begins to occur. We must pray and purpose in our hearts to seek His presence to fill every office, school classroom, restaurant, jail cell, nursing home, and sports arena in our communities!

## 5. Empire Building to Kingdom Building

With the newfound hope that God wants to bring transformation to our entire community, we can begin to see the futility of building our own "empires." Because true kingdom vision is so overwhelming and larger than any individual ministry can carry, we are now more willing to lay down our own agendas and work together for God's purposes in our cities. This is one of our biggest challenges for believers in the Western world—our fascination and love of building things. We're good at it! Unfortunately, our skill in building can make us more impressed with what *we* are building than what the Lord wants to build. Until we see the big picture and the lack of fruit in the face of the devastation facing us, we will remain satisfied with our own agendas and empire building.

## 6. Workers to Lovers

God is drawing His church back to intimacy with Him and challenging our ministry-based identities. As the realization of the love of God begins to restore and transform us, our motivation shifts from being a "worker" for God to being a "lover" of God. We move from the pressure of a performance-based mentality to a rest and contentment in being loved and then serve out of that love. This is bringing a tremendous sense of rest to the body of Christ—we don't have to perform to be loved! We are loved, therefore, we love, and that becomes our ministry expression. After all, we are human *beings,* right? Not human *doings!*

## 7. Warriors to Worshipers

A very important shift in recent years is our understanding of the role of intercession. Many intercessors have grown weary and even wounded by an overemphasis of "warring" against the enemy. As the message of intimacy seeps into the mind of the body of Christ we are gratefully sitting at His feet like Mary and then interceding out of our intimate fellowship with our King. There is certainly a reality of spiritual warfare that we are involved in, but our gaze must remain focused on Jesus. When we worship Him, the spiritual atmosphere around us changes because the Bible says, "God inhabits the praises" of His people (Ps. 22:3). When the presence of God is manifest it displaces the kingdom of darkness.

## 8. "Sacred" Versus "Secular" to Kingdom Focused

In contrast to the clergy-only approach to citywide ministry, the Lord is beginning to connect other spiritual leaders together in our cities. The wall of separation between the "sacred" and the "secular" is breaking down. Christian leaders in the marketplace, political and educational systems are connecting to kingdom purposes and extending the influence of the kingdom of God beyond the walls of the local church. The church is not a building or an institution! Being part of the church means to be part of the body of Christ, and that is a mobile family unit. We need to recognize the full expression of the body and release all Christians to minister into their communities. Most people who need Jesus don't come into the local congregations to hear a sermon on Sundays; they need contact with a "minister of reconciliation" on Tuesday mornings and Friday evenings as well!

God is raising up people that represent the fullness of His kingdom—men and women who are multiethnic, multigenerational, multivocational Jews and Gentiles. We are beginning to see the various giftings and callings of believers expressed not only

> THE CHURCH IS NOT A BUILDING OR AN INSTITUTION!

inside the walls of the church buildings but also out in the community.

## 9. Methods of Man to Presence of God

Once we have tired of our endless attempts to produce lasting fruit from fleshly ideas, we begin to wait more on the Lord. There is a very healthy frustration in the church right now with man-made programs and methods. As a result, we are longing for reality and a deeper connection to Jesus. We are turning away from our busyness and preoccupations to seek Him. Spending time in prayer and waiting on the Lord produce humility and wisdom. He purifies our character as we spend time in His presence. When we are willing to acknowledge that our own wisdom and ideas aren't as fruitful as the Lord's, we will be willing to wait on Him.

## 10. Being "Experts" to Becoming "Learners"

One of the challenges of the Western world is how many self-described "experts" we have in the church. Everybody is an expert! After a reality check about our condition, however, you can't help but wonder: "experts at what?" With such a high value placed on knowledge in the West, we tend to think since we "know" about something, we are experts in the field. The evidence suggests that while we may be *educated* in the ways of God, we aren't currently *walking out* those principles with a great deal of fruitfulness.

By contrast, the testimonies of how God is moving through His church in power and effectiveness in nation after nation in the non-Western world are mind-boggling! Signs and wonders are happening, revival is spreading, thousands of people are getting saved, and cities are being turned upside down by God's transforming power. Who is leading this movement? Nobody you would probably know or recognize. They don't have platform ministries or bestselling books. The leaders God is raising up in the nations aren't well-known, but they are well-schooled in the ways of God.

God's ways are so much higher than our ways! Paul describes God's "modus operandi" this way:

> But God has chosen the foolish things of the world to put to shame the wise, and God has chosen the weak things of the world to put to shame the things which are mighty; and the base things of the world and the things which are despised God has chosen, and the things which are not, to bring to nothing the things that are, that no flesh should glory in His presence. (1 Corinthians 1:27–29)

We need to posture ourselves in humility and learn from leaders in the nations who have a story to tell! The overwhelming evidence of our condition should cause us to position ourselves as "learners" rather than experts. We are in a position of weakness not strength, and humility is our only hope of moving out of our current condition.

## THE POWER AND WISDOM OF SIMPLICITY

It might seem logical that in order to participate with God in such a lofty vision as transformation we would need a highly intellectual, organized, and complicated plan. But from what I have studied in God's Word and experienced in real life testimony, it's actually quite the opposite. Our plans and human wisdom *get in God's way* and interfere with the powerful simplicity of the kingdom of God.

A. W. Tozer says it this way:

> If we would find God amid all the religious externals, we must first determine to find Him, and then proceed in the way of simplicity. Now, as always, God discovers Himself to "babes" and hides Himself in thick darkness from the wise and the prudent. We must simplify our approach to Him. We must strip down to essentials (and they will be found to be blessedly few). We must put away all effort to impress, and come with the guileless candor of childhood. If we do this, without doubt God will quickly respond.[3]

God's ways simply aren't our ways and His thoughts aren't our thoughts! God is capable of understanding everything in time and history—each person's callings and giftings, every detail of every need in the city, and the best way to work it out for everybody concerned. Then He orchestrates His plans according to His own wisdom and timing. We can't begin to understand such things, but we can be obedient to His Word and live according to His kingdom values.

True success is living a life of faithful obedience to Jesus, and that need not be complicated. What it lacks in complication will be made up for in passion!

> TRUE SUCCESS IS LIVING A LIFE OF FAITHFUL OBEDIENCE TO JESUS, AND THAT NEED NOT BE COMPLICATED. WHAT IT LACKS IN COMPLICATION WILL BE MADE UP FOR IN PASSION!

## Chapter 13

# RESTORATION OF GOD'S PRESENCE

"LET US BE GLAD AND REJOICE AND GIVE HIM
GLORY, FOR THE MARRIAGE OF THE LAMB HAS
COME, AND HIS WIFE HAS
MADE HERSELF READY."

REVELATION 19:7

The ultimate goal of all redemption is to prepare a bride for God's perfect Son. The corporate church is even now in preparation for a wedding, the day when the Spirit and the bride will say, "Come!" (Rev. 22:17). From before the foundation of the world to the threshold of eternity, God has been planning and preparing for this grand event—the glorious wedding of His Son—the marriage supper of the Lamb.

Everything in Scripture and all of history is moving toward this one grand finale, when redeemed humanity will be united in eternal fellowship with Jesus. We must understand this final outcome if we are going to understand the meaning and purpose of history and how we fit into the big picture. We have history's final chapter in the book of Revelation. The ultimate outcome and goal of all the events from eternity to eternity, the finished product of all the ages, is the spotless bride of Christ!

This understanding must be the context and compass for everything else we do. The eternal companion of Jesus will sit with Him on His throne (Revelation 3:21). We, as part of the bride of Christ, are participating in this preparation.

How does this glorious goal and conclusion affect us now? An important reality of the kingdom of God is that it is both a future reality and a "here and now" reality. This means that we don't live our lives in compromise and captivity and then one day everything changes supernaturally into the new, glorious reality. God gives us glimpses and deposits of eternity and His kingdom right now, if we have eyes to see and ears to hear. We must be people who are living with a heavenly perspective, bringing Jesus glory by partnering with Him in His purposes on the earth right now!

The Word of God in the New Testament teaches that God himself is preparing for His bride a new city, the New Jerusalem. It is described as a place where Jesus reigns in justice, where sin and death are removed, where the land flourishes, and the nations are healed.

## The Bride—Many Nations, Many Tribes

God has promised His Son Jesus the nations as His inheritance (Psalm 2:7–8). His spotless bride will be formed from every tribe and tongue. We see the fulfillment of this promise in Revelation 7:9–10:

> After these things I looked, and behold, a great multitude which no one could number, of all nations, tribes, peoples, and tongues, standing before the throne and before the Lamb, clothed with white robes, with palm branches in their hands, and crying out with a loud voice, saying, "Salvation to our God who sits on the throne and to the Lamb!"

Hundreds of people groups, every language and color imaginable, will form the bride! She will be beautiful and spotless; she will be unified and reflect His glory.

We see another picture of the bride of Christ in Revelation:

> "Come! I will show you the bride, the Lamb's wife." And he carried me away in the Spirit to a great and high mountain, and showed me the great city, the holy Jerusalem descending out of heaven from God, having the glory of God. And her light was like a most precious stone, like a jasper stone, clear as crystal. (Revelation 21:9–11)

Isn't it interesting that the bride is pictured here as a city? The bride is not the structures of the city but the people in the city, the corporate bride. In the New Jerusalem, there will be no temple or sun because the presence and glory of God illuminates it (Revelation 21:23). The Lamb is its light. She is described as a city made of precious stones and gold as transparent as glass that will reflect the glory of the Lord with unimaginable brilliance. No wonder the nations and kings of the earth will gather there (v. 25)!

The New Jerusalem is a picture of how the corporate church is supposed to be functioning now spiritually. We as the living stones from every tribe and tongue must be built together to become a dwelling place for God in our cities! The bride of Christ won't be comprised of only Scandinavian Lutherans, Texan Baptists, English Anglicans, or Brazilian Pentecostals!

## Restoration of God's Presence

How do we prepare for this glorious outcome of history? Do we just sit by and watch it unfold? Or do we live in the reality of God's purposes right now by committing ourselves to passionately pursue Him? I believe God is inviting us to partner with Him in the preparation of His bride and the salvation of the nations!

> THE RESTORATION OF GOD'S MANIFEST PRESENCE IN THE LIVES OF GOD'S PEOPLE WILL RESULT IN THE RESTORATION OF GOD'S GLORY.

We begin by returning to the life-giving covenant God has extended to us, and we prepare ourselves to be a dwelling place for God's presence in our communities. The restoration of God's manifest presence in the lives of God's people will result in the restoration of God's glory. God's desire and purpose is that His glory be displayed openly "in the church and in Christ Jesus throughout all generations, for ever and ever!" (Eph. 3:21 NIV). What would that look like? Ezekiel describes this glorious return of God's glory like the roar of rushing waters:

> I saw the glory of the God of Israel coming from the east. His voice was like the roar of rushing waters, and the land was radiant with His glory. (43:2)

The return of God's presence and glory is also described in Ezekiel 47 as being like that of a river that began to flow from the temple outward. At first the river of God's life-giving presence began as a trickle, then it became ankle deep; it got progressively deeper until it was a mighty river that could not be crossed. The river flowed to the dry, dead, and desolate places. Everywhere the river flowed, life sprang forth, fruitfulness occurred, and healing happened. The river in Ezekiel is a prophetic picture of God's presence flowing out of His temple, the people of God, to bring life and healing to cities and nations.

A similar picture appears in Revelation, where the river of God flows from the throne and down the middle of the streets of the city, bringing healing and life. Jesus, the Lamb of God, is in the middle of the city, illuminating it with the light of His presence (Revelation 22).

The transformation of a community is a journey, not an overnight success. It takes time for God's presence to be restored as the defining reality of a community. This journey is like the river in Ezekiel, it begins as a stream and then increases little by little as it grows and deepens, touching and healing everything in its path. First it touches the people of God, and then through them the river of God flows out into their workplaces and neighborhoods, bringing life and healing to the city.

## RESTORATION OF PRESENCE IN THE CHURCH

What does it look like when the tangible presence of Jesus is restored to His church? The best example we have is the fruit of His ministry when He walked on the earth. Jesus is light and life! Wherever Jesus went, He brought light into the darkness and life to barren souls. What must that

> THE TRANSFORMATION OF A COMMUNITY IS A JOURNEY, NOT AN OVERNIGHT SUCCESS.

have been like—to be with Jesus as He healed a paralytic or a sick child; when He stopped by to minister to the Samaritan woman or raise Lazarus from the dead; or to listen to Him teach on the hillside or on the boat off the shore of the sea?

When the presence of Jesus is restored in a tangible way, He will restore light and life to His church, impacting us in three critical ways:

## 1. Spiritual Identity:

When we experience the tangible presence of Jesus, it stirs a hunger in us to know Him. Then our love for Him will lead us into the quiet place of personal transformation. Those encounters with Jesus will restore us to our first love and true identity. As we grow in our knowledge of the Lord, spiritual reality will wash away the rhetoric and veneer of our Christian life. You cannot spend time in His presence and not be transformed!

As we grow in increased intimacy with the Lord, we will grow in our understanding of the importance of our corporate identity as His church and our interdependence upon the body of Christ. We will also begin to understand our role as the "priesthood of believers" and rejoice in partnering with Jesus in prayer for others.

Another aspect of our identity as believers is not only to be filled with God's glory but also to become "releasers" of it to people around us. The river of God must flow through us. It has an origination point (the throne room of God) and a destination (the people in our communities). We are called to be "ministers of reconciliation" and to release God's glory on the earth. It's not given to us for preservation or maintenance purposes! We must carry His presence like light into dark places. God's glory is meant to fill His people and be poured out as an offering to a thirsty community.

## 2. Spiritual Authority:

When the fire of God's presence is restored, He will burn away the dross in our lives and give us gold that has been refined by the fire. The enemies of compromise and complacency will be rooted out of us, the shame of our nakedness will be covered with pure garments, and we will regain our spiritual eyesight (Revelation 3:18). Then our former spiritual condition will become abhorrent and rightly viewed as an enemy of God. People who have been delivered out of their own sin and compromise will become deliverers for many others! Passion for Jesus will become the highest priority of our lives.

When the church is restored to holiness and righteousness, her spiritual authority, once weakened by compromise, will also be restored. The church will reflect the nature and character of Jesus, and when His name is spoken, it will have impact and not be ridiculed. The power of God will be released through His church just like it was in the book of Acts and in the testimonies of transforming revival throughout church history.

Daniel 11:32 says that the people who know their God "shall be strong, and carry out great exploits." When people know who they are in God and who God is in them, they will be stirred to boldly proclaim the gospel! The Word of God will be preached with power and fruitful results (John 15). People will be gripped by the Word and come under the conviction of the Holy Spirit, enabling them to commit their hearts to Jesus.

In the face of persecution, Paul prayed for this very thing in Acts, chapter 4:

> "Now, Lord, look on their threats, and grant to Your servants that with all boldness they may speak Your word, by stretching out Your hand to heal, and that signs and wonders may be done by the name of Your holy Servant Jesus." And when they had prayed, the place was shaken where they were assembled together; and they were all filled with the Holy Spirit, and they spoke the word of God with boldness. (Acts 4:29–31)

Imagine a prayer meeting where the room you were meeting in was literally shaken! That encounter with God filled them with the Spirit, and they preached the Word with boldness. Jesus is inviting us to the same lifestyle of simple obedience, sacrifice, and demonstration of the power of God in our ministry.

### 3. Transforming Purpose:

As God's presence is restored to His church and strongholds are broken, the people of God will become free from compromise and self-serving agendas to become a counterculture and agents of change in our communities.

When we grow in our love for Jesus, we will begin to understand our transforming purpose. Then we will turn from our self-centered and independent agendas and begin to love and serve the city where

God has placed us. We are called to love it together and to covenant with God for its restoration. The church will impact cities and nations "not by might nor by power," but by His Spirit! (Zechariah 4:6).

Demonic influence over our cities will be uprooted as the church enforces the spiritual authority entrusted to her. In their place, God will bring restoration and healing to the captives, those who mourn, and the brokenhearted (Isaiah 61:1).

When Jesus becomes the preeminent attraction in His church, He will "draw all men" to himself (John 12:32). Hungry souls will flock to encounter Jesus dwelling in His body, and the prayer of Jesus in John 17 will be answered.

God's restored presence among us provides hope for our purpose and destiny. When His presence is a present-tense reality, He can lead us by His voice and guide us by His eye. A church that is restored and revived can then carry God's presence and glory into the community. We must consider the resources of heaven that Jesus makes available to us, and take those heavenly resources to our cities.

## THE FRUIT OF RESTORED PRESENCE—TRANSFORMATION!

When God's manifest presence and favor begin to return to a community, restoration and healing can occur. The goal of the restoration of God's presence in His church is that our city will be transformed from its ruined condition to become a reflection of God's glory and beauty:

> You [Jerusalem] shall also be a *crown of glory in the hand of the Lord, and a royal diadem in the hand of your God.* You shall no longer be termed Forsaken, nor shall your land any more be termed Desolate; but you shall be called Hephzibah, and your land Beulah; for the Lord delights in you, and your land shall be married. For as a young man marries a virgin, so shall your sons marry you; and as the bridegroom rejoices over the bride, so shall your God rejoice over you. (Isaiah 62:3–4, emphasis added)

What does it mean for a city to become a "crown of glory in the hand of the Lord"? First and most obviously, the crown indicates royalty. The crown belongs to a King and He is the King of a kingdom. The kingdom of God supercedes everything else. A "crowned" city is an indication of His kingdom having touched the earth. It means that God has found a faithful people to covenant with for His restoration purposes.

The crown isn't something worn by the institutions of the city; it's something the city reflects as a result of the transforming work of God among His people. Israel dwelling in the city of Jerusalem becomes God's "crown," which He holds in His hands before the nations to declare their worth before God.

In the Old Testament, there are two main definitions for the Hebrew word *crown*. First is *nezer*, which means to "set something apart, or consecrate, as when a person is dedicated to the priesthood, or becomes royalty." It comes from the root word *nazar*, meaning to "hold aloof from impurity and to be set apart for sacred purposes."[1]

The second use of the word *crown* in the Old Testament is the Hebrew word *atarah*, which was used as a crown of exaltation, honor, and victory. It comes from the root *atar*, meaning "to encircle as in war for protection or defense."[2]

A city that becomes a "crown of glory" is a city that is consecrated or set apart to the Lord for His purposes, a city with an uncompromised church that is reflecting God's glory. It's a city where the church is victorious, the house of the Lord is established, and His presence is tangible in their midst, offering the protection of His presence. It's a city where the priests are watching and guarding the city and contending for God's presence, a place where the lost can look at the church and see Jesus and His power at work in life-changing ways.

In Zechariah we read, "The Lord their God will save them in that day, as the flock of His people. For they shall be *like the jewels of a crown*, lifted like a banner over His land" (Zech. 9:16, emphasis added). Individual believers are the jewels (living stones) that get set into the crown, adorning the bride in the city.

What an amazing promise! Imagine a city being called "Forsaken" and then being renamed *Hephzibah* because the Lord delights in her! Imagine a city that had been called "Desolate" and is renamed *Beulah* because the land is "married" as part of God's covenant promise with His people! The city was literally renamed to reflect the new identity God had given to her.

What is your city known for? Do you have a reputation for something? Is it a reputation that glorifies the Lord? When God's presence and glory become a present-tense reality, the church in the city will become alive with life and purpose!

While this passage in Isaiah 62 refers to the ultimate restoration of Jerusalem, this is also a reflection of God's heart for our cities. The promises and covenants made to Israel in the Old Testament are first specific to her as a nation and people. God chose and made covenant with Israel to be His people in order that His glory might be shown through them as a light to the Gentile cities and nations. In addition, God's covenant with Israel as a nation represents His heart for His full bride, made up of both Jewish and Gentile believers.

Like many other Scriptures, this passage is a depiction of God's nature and character to offer covenant relationship with people dwelling in cities. God longs to bring healing and restoration to forsaken cities, whether that city is Jerusalem, Hong Kong, or Chicago! It's just who He is. God's nature is to heal brokenness, deliver captives, and gather wandering people to himself.

## CITIES WITH A NEW IDENTITY

Jesus came to set us free, to save us from sin, and to give us abundant life. He not only intended that reality to affect us personally but also corporately. Jesus has much more in mind than personal salvation for individuals and blessing for His church; His plan includes bringing salvation, restoration, and transformation to multitudes of people, cities, and nations before He returns (see Ezekiel 47:9, 12; Revelation 7:9, 14)!

It isn't possible to know our true identity until we meet Jesus. Through salvation, we gain access to a new nature and destiny. The same is true for our cities. When Jesus is invited into our communities, He brings salvation, healing, and right identity. Today cities are known for many things—sports teams, monuments, and various activities. In the case of communities that have been transformed, their reputation has been changed from one of vice and brokenness to one that displays restoration, healing, and prosperity!

Genuine revival and transformation will result in restored identity in both the church and the community. Then the actual reputation of the city will change as a result of the testimony of Jesus and His life-transforming power at work among the people.

The primary reason God restores and transforms people and communities is to be glorified in them! In the Scriptures, we see numerous examples of God changing a community and therefore her very identity and reputation. God promises through Jeremiah to restore both Israel and Judah and to restore the city of Jerusalem as well. Jeremiah says,

> Then this city will bring me renown, joy, praise and honor before all nations on earth that hear of all the good things I do for it; and they will be in awe and will tremble at the abundant prosperity and peace I provide for it. (33:9 NIV)

Isaiah prophesies about this same restoring transformation: "The nations will see your righteousness, and all kings your glory; you will be called by a new name that the mouth of the Lord will bestow" (62:2).

The Word of God speaks about cities becoming a "praise on the earth" (Isa. 62:7); cities being renamed "The Lord Is There" (Ezek. 48:35); and the "City of the Lord" (Isa. 60:14). Only the Lord can give a new name and identity, because the new name He gives expresses the transformation work He has done among the people.

Jesus, in His letter to the church of Philadelphia, encouraged them with the following:

> "I am coming soon. Hold on to what you have, so that no one will take your crown. I will write on him the name of my God and the name of the city of my God, the new Jerusalem, which is coming down out of heaven. And I will also write on him my new name" (Revelation 3:11–12 NIV).

Clearly, cities can experience redeeming change and transformation because of the manifest presence and grace of God expressed through His Son Jesus!

## A DESPERATE CITY UNLOCKED FOR TRANSFORMATION!

If you have ever traveled to a Third World country one of the first things you witness is the level of visible desperation in the people. And when you encounter God's people in these countries, they are typically just as desperate for spiritual things as they are physically desperate.

I certainly found that to be true on my first ministry trip to Russia. We were shocked at the absolute desperation for God and determination of the people of God to pursue Him. They wanted Jesus to come to their city! People would come from all over and sit through six hours of teaching in one afternoon and still be hungry for more! They were also the happiest people I have ever met, despite the fact that each one had either lived through or was living in extremely difficult circumstances.

Samara is a city of two million people located five hundred miles east of Moscow. During World War II, Samara became a top-secret military manufacturing base, and therefore most of the people worked for the war industry. As is common in Russia, the whole mindset of the people was to prepare for and survive war—it's all they have ever known.

Decades of living in secrecy as a military city have taken their toll on Samara. Most men are alcoholics and die before they are fifty years old. The divorce rate is over 65 percent. Drug addiction among the youth is common. There is little food, much poverty, no recreation, and little or no ability to support a family. Although capitalism has replaced communism, the people have not made a successful transition to this new form of government. So people must plant gardens outside the city and grow their own food. The city government, including the police department and court system, is corrupt and still influenced by the Russian Mafia. Fear—and suspicion of those in authority—permeates life.

In addition to the city, the church in Samara was also in "ruins." When we arrived the evangelical churches there were only ten years old and had grown up in a context of brokenness. Bitterness and disunity ranked high among the churches, and little trust existed between the leaders and their congregations or among leaders citywide. Everyone was simply trying to survive in their devastated culture.

In the midst of the trauma and hopelessness, however, a faithful remnant of people cried out in desperation to God, and in 1993 several pastors from a group of churches in Indiana began sowing in the

Samara region by planting churches. On their first trip to the city, hundreds of people were saved and many miracles occurred, including the healing of the blind, deaf, and lame, stirring faith and hope in Samara that God had indeed heard their cry. Pastors Ray Renner, Johnny Cawthon, Bob Combs, and others began revisiting the city two or three times per year, teaching, encouraging, and strengthening them. Then the Lord led two young women from South Africa, Erica and Miranda, to move to Samara and start a Bible institute. Once the Bible institute began in 2001 the students devoted the opening of every school day to a period of intercession for Samara and other countries around the world.

In 2002 Erica and Miranda sold their only vehicle to buy plane tickets so they could come to the United States and visit their friends in Indiana. They also wanted to visit the International House of Prayer in Kansas City. I was anxious to meet them—having heard such amazing stories about them—so we had coffee. Within five minutes I was so gripped by God's favor on them and the passion of their hearts to see revival come to their city that I agreed to their invitation to come to Samara and teach on city transformation. I found myself traveling to Samara for ten days of ministry in early 2003. The week began with a City Transformation Conference, and more than half of the pastors in the city and people from their congregations participated.

On the first day of the conference I ministered from Isaiah 62:4–5. I told the crowd gathered that God had invited His people into a covenant relationship with Him and that part of His covenant to "marry" them included healing and restoration for their own lives as well as for their city. I shared other Scriptures with them, including Isaiah 61, which promises that "they will rebuild ruined cities and the desolations of many generations."

As we had been talking about God's desire to covenant with His people, I sensed the Lord leading me to ask a pointed question. He wanted them to enter into His covenant and partner with Him to bring restoration to this broken city. So I asked them the question I heard from the Lord: "Who will marry Samara?" I repeated it again: "Who will marry Samara?"

Because of the cultural and language barriers, I had no idea if they understood anything I had said in the previous six hours. And I knew the terminology I was using was a bit unusual. Did they understand the meaning of it? Had I communicated adequately what I sensed was on the Lord's heart? What followed next amazed me. The people began to stand and cry out to God, shouting, "I will! I will!" as a declaration of their love and commitment to the Lord and to their city. Suddenly a groundswell of God's presence swept the room as His people responded to His invitation. With newfound hope the people turned toward the windows in the meeting room that looked out over the city. Taking their Bibles, they began to read every promise they could find in the Word and declared it over the city: "Samara, you are no longer forsaken!" "God rejoices over you!" "Samara, you have a hope and a future!"

As they spoke life and blessing over the city, I knew hope was coming to the broken lives, corrupt institutions, barren land, and desperate families. God had pierced the hearts of His faithful remnant and they responded to His invitation to take spiritual responsibility for their ruined city.

This continued for about thirty minutes. After blessing the city, we worshiped together and rejoiced over what the Lord had done that day. We hugged one another and wept. We tried to close the meeting several times, but the Lord had drawn the people into His presence in such a powerful way that they didn't want to stop worshiping Him. That was the first time the family of God had ever worshiped together in the city—and they loved it!

As soon as I stepped outside the building late that afternoon I sensed a change in the spiritual atmosphere. What had felt dark, oppressive, and hopeless just hours before now seemed filled with hope and light. As we walked back out into the streets of the city from our "upper room" experience with Jesus, it felt as if life were being poured back into the city. Life was returning to Samara because God's covenant with His people was being restored.

After the initial breakthrough the Lord continued to do mighty things during the following week. Pastors repented publicly for their control and independence and agreed to meet and pray together. (They continue to do so a year later.) The corporate identity of the body of Christ took root in the hearts of believers and the presence of the Lord was experienced in many tangible ways.

In the months following our visit the spiritual climate over the city changed and many experienced healing from physical afflictions. These reports caused a local hospital to send people to the Bible Institute to be prayed for! The message of covenant and hope has also been transported by Bible Institute students back to their own villages, with powerful results. Despite great darkness and difficult circumstances that continue to face the people of Samara, the people of God are seeing the house of the Lord being established to bring hope to a once-desolate city.

## CITIES OF REFUGE

When a city becomes a "crown of glory in the hand of the Lord," it becomes a shelter for the people dwelling in it, a place of refuge. It becomes a city that is protected and defended against the enemy and is transformed from "desolate" to "married." When the presence of the Lord is in a city, it becomes a refuge, because the Lord is dwelling among His people.

In the Old Testament, God made provision for Israel to have six cities designated as "cities of refuge" for those who had committed manslaughter (Deuteronomy 19). The law required that when somebody was killed, the nearest family member was required to take revenge on the person responsible. This person was referred to as the "avenger of blood." Under the old covenant, there was no provision to ransom murderers (Numbers 35:31). Their only protection was to seek shelter in a "city of refuge" until justice could be determined.

We can draw a spiritual application from this idea in the Old Testament for what God has in mind for our cities today. Under the New Covenant, forgiveness of sin has been made possible for us through Jesus Christ. We are literally delivered from the "avenger" when we are redeemed, because Jesus made the ultimate sacrifice, paying for our sins with His own blood. We, as His body, are then to be "reconcilers" of people to God—extending the good news of the gospel and inviting them to also seek refuge in Him.

Deuteronomy 33:37 says, "The eternal God is your refuge, and underneath are the everlasting arms. He will thrust out the enemy from before you, and will say, 'Destroy!'" Then in Psalm 91:2 we read, "I will say of the Lord, 'He is my refuge and fortress; my God, in Him I will trust.'"

"They wandered in the wilderness in a desolate way; they found no city to dwell in. Hungry and thirsty, their soul fainted in them. Then they cried out to the Lord in their trouble, and He delivered them out of their distresses. And He led them forth by the right way, that they might go to a city for a dwelling place" (Psalm 107:4–7).

What would your city look like if it became a spiritual and socially redeemed "city of refuge"? Can wandering souls find His tangible presence in your church and community? Are they safe from the "avenger" in your city or subject to destruction and violence?

Transformed communities are cities of spiritual and social refuge, where enemies such as poverty, addictions, and violence have been defeated and the once-forsaken city has become safe and prosperous. The avenger is not allowed to enter, because the gatekeepers are at the gates and the watchmen are on the walls. People running from the enemy and their own sin can find salvation and protection in the presence of God.

## A WEDDING PRESENT FOR JESUS

We must become desperate for God's presence, because only He can empower us to pursue the restoration and transformation of our cities. God wants to restore devastated places and bring life so that our city or community becomes a shelter and a refuge for the people He loves.

Can our cities become "crowns of glory in the hand of the Lord," a place where He is worshiped and glorified, where His bride is in covenant with her Bridegroom and with the land of her inheritance? Even now the bride is being prepared for the Bridegroom! What can we give Jesus of greater value than ourselves and the city He has entrusted to our care?

Could that be a "wedding present" that we, the bride, will give to our Bridegroom on that day—a "crowned city"—one that has been redeemed, restored, renamed, and filled with His glory? As we earnestly pray for the revival of God's manifest presence in the church and the restoration of God's redeeming, transforming purpose in our city, let us do so with a clear goal in mind—that our city will become "a praise on the earth," a place of spiritual refuge.

And they shall call them The Holy People, the Redeemed of the Lord; and you shall be called Sought Out, a City Not Forsaken. (Isaiah 62:12)

Chapter 14

# DESPERATION: THE KEY
# TO TRANSFORMATION

"OH, THAT YOU WOULD REND THE HEAVENS
AND COME DOWN, THAT THE MOUNTAINS
WOULD TREMBLE BEFORE YOU! AS WHEN FIRE
SETS TWIGS ABLAZE AND CAUSES WATER TO BOIL,
COME DOWN TO MAKE YOUR NAME KNOWN TO
YOUR ENEMIES AND CAUSE THE NATIONS TO
QUAKE BEFORE YOU! FOR WHEN YOU DID
AWESOME THINGS THAT WE DID NOT EXPECT,
YOU CAME DOWN, AND THE MOUNTAINS
TREMBLED BEFORE YOU. SINCE ANCIENT TIMES
NO ONE HAS HEARD, NO EAR HAS PERCEIVED,
NO EYE HAS SEEN ANY GOD BESIDES YOU,
WHO ACTS ON BEHALF OF THOSE
WHO WAIT FOR HIM."

ISAIAH 64:1–4 (NIV)

Can you feel the sense of expectancy in Isaiah's message? He says the very earth will be affected—"mountains will tremble" before Him and the "nations will quake"—when God steps down from heaven! God is going to do awesome things, things we cannot fully imagine.

I hope that God has stirred your heart as we've looked at the condition of the Western church and the absolute necessity of contending for the presence of Jesus to be restored among us. As we've looked at the factors that can either attract His presence or cause Him to remain at a distance, has it resulted in a longing in your heart to want to build a dwelling place for Him? Have you wondered, "How can we prepare our community for God's habitation?" What about the condition of the dwelling place in your own heart?

Are you gripped by the reality that God has more for you than pleasant, predictable worship services? Are you in a place of captivity—overrun by all the things that caused the children of Israel to become captives to a pagan culture? Or has God already called you into a wilderness place—to renew your covenant with Him and to prepare you for personal and corporate revival? Are you beginning to understand the awesome responsibility that He has given to us, His church, to be gatekeepers, reconcilers, and agents of change within our cities and communities? Can you feel God's heart for the lost and are you excited to be a part of bringing them to Jesus?

The promise and potential for a community to be transformed already exists in the heart of God. As we grow in our intimacy with Jesus, His heart becomes our heart and He shares His secrets and plans with us—His beloved. As we mature in our faith and relationship with the Lord, He will entrust wisdom, understanding, and revelation to us to fulfill His purposes. Jesus said, "I will give you the keys of the kingdom of heaven" (Matt. 16:19). We get these "keys" only through intimate relationship with the Lord.

Whoever has been given a key, possesses the authority to use it. If I have a key to my house, I have the authority of legitimate entry. But without the appropriate key, the door doesn't open. When things are not opening spiritually, we should ask ourselves:

> MAN-MADE KEYS DON'T UNLOCK HEAVEN'S DOORS!

"Do we have the right key?" Man-made keys don't unlock heaven's doors!

We must use spiritual principles in His Word as "keys" to unlock our hearts individually and prepare as a church for God's habitation. There are a number of spiritual principles that serve as keys in the transformation process. We've discussed these in other chapters. Here is a brief summary:

- *Unity among God's people*—not just for doing things together once in a while, but a deep sense of our interdependence and connectedness. As the collective expression of God's church in a region our unity must be tangible and organic.
- *Love and humility*—these must mark all we do in the name of Jesus with and for others. Love for God is our first priority; love for our fellowman flows from that.
- *Repentance*—as we recognize how far we have wandered from God and how far short we fall in terms of representing Him to the world around us, we use 2 Chronicles 7:14 as a guide for returning to covenant with God.
- *Intimacy with Christ*—enables us to take up our unique role in the world as the bride and body of Christ. As royal priests unto our God we gain the spiritual authority needed to see revival and city transformation become a reality.

Notice that these keys are not activities or plans of action. They are concerned with the condition of our hearts, our character, our "being" rather than our "doing." That's because we must be conformed to the image of Christ before we can minister life to those around us. Busyness does not necessarily build the kingdom of God!

This doesn't mean that we shouldn't be strategic or have ministry plans. The point is that until the presence of Jesus is restored to His church and to the city, our ministry plans aren't sufficient. It's simply a matter of ordering our priorities—Jesus first, ministry second. When the body of Christ is restored to covenant relationship and intimate fellowship with the Lord, He will lead us in many creative, effective ministry expressions that will have an abundance of fruit. Ministering to people is God's idea! His presence guarantees effectiveness.

I happen to be a strategic thinker. I love ministry strategy, and through the years the Lord has allowed me to serve cities with a measure of wisdom and revelation from His heart. I do believe the Lord has wisdom hidden in His heart that is prepared for us (1 Corinthians 2:7), and that as we seek Him He will reveal it in accordance with His purposes. But this isn't earthly wisdom, because "No one knows the things of God except the Spirit of God" (1 Cor. 2:11). Spiritual things must be spiritually discerned.

Our plans and ministry strategies can originate from heaven if we seek the Lord in prayer with utter dependence and humility. The questions we must ask ourselves regarding a new ministry plan are "Where did we get it?" "Is the strategy something that God gave to us together in prayer?" "Was it born of God's Spirit or of the flesh?"

We have to lay a new foundation for ministry in the Western church if we are going to expect more fruitfulness. We cannot ignore foundational issues, such as identity, unity, humility, and persevering prayer any longer. If we do establish this new foundation, with Jesus as the Cornerstone, we can build a dwelling place for God's presence in our cities. Then the expression of ministry in the body of Christ will become life-giving, powerful, and earth-changing! And, I might add, a lot more enjoyable!

## PREPARING FOR TRANSFORMATION

Jesus gives us a clear picture in Revelation, when He addresses the Laodicean church about the spiritual journey that prepares us for transformation. First, Jesus points out their double-mindedness and the reality of their condition and offers them counsel to be delivered from their compromise. He then encourages them by saying, "As many as I love, I rebuke and chasten. Therefore be zealous and repent" (3:19).

Jesus wants us to understand the reality of our spiritual condition so we can (1) repent of our compromised condition; and (2) be restored by taking His counsel (to be refined in the fire, put on new garments of holiness, and apply eye salve so that we can see).

Then we see Jesus standing at the door of His church knocking, waiting to be invited back in. If Jesus is knocking on the door it is because He is on the *outside,* not the inside!

> "Behold, I stand at the door and knock. If anyone hears My voice and opens the door, I will come in to him and dine with him, and he with Me" (Revelation 3:20).

We can't produce transformation in our communities any more than we can produce transformation in ourselves. It's a process that requires humbling ourselves before the Lord and seeking Him with our whole heart until the very nature of Christ is formed within us—

personally and corporately. While we cannot write a plan for transformation, we can and should earnestly pray and prepare for it. We start by opening the door and inviting Jesus back into His church!

## THE WORK OF WAITING

"No one has heard, no ear has perceived, no eye has seen any God besides you, who acts on behalf of those who wait for Him" (Isa. 64:4 NIV). This Scripture promises that God will act on behalf of those who "wait for Him." Waiting is not passive; it's an active pressing in to the Lord with hearts filled with holy desire and prophetic expectancy. It's the same idea as the parable Jesus told of the ten virgins. They all waited for the bridegroom to come but only five of them were prepared, having their lamps trimmed and filled with oil.

You might wonder, "If we are going to see all these amazing things in our cities, how can we wait—don't we need to be *doing* something?" That is a fair question. How we answer that question will determine how we proceed and how effective we will be on the journey of transformation.

The tendency in the Western world is overwhelmingly to "do something." Waiting is almost unthinkable to some people; they equate it with wasting time. But if we believe that ministry requires the presence of Jesus in the midst of His church why would we do anything but wait for His presence to come? Can we tarry *until. . . ?*

Waiting on the Lord is fruitful, *not* unfruitful. Spending time in His presence enables us to connect with Him and gain understanding about His nature, His Word, and His heart. That communion forms us into His image. We must be zealous and passionate, prepared in every way, aware of the urgency of the hour, abandoned to the call, and filled with God's presence; then we wait!

When the shaking begins it's too late to think about building a place of refuge and shelter in our cities. It's imperative that the church prepare a dwelling place for the Lord *now*. It's critical that our cities become places of refuge *now*. Otherwise we will be like the five foolish virgins who found themselves unprepared for the bridegroom's return. When he came, it was too late to fill their lamps with oil.

And it will be said in that day, "Behold, this is our God; we have waited for Him; we will be glad and rejoice in His salvation" (Isa.

25:9). This is in contrast to the message Jesus brings to the Ephesian church (Revelation 2:2–4) when He said that they had been very busy but had lost their first love.

Information doesn't transform cities. Conferences can't transform a city! Education can't transform a city! Having citywide ministry programs or large networks cannot transform a city. Only the presence of Jesus can bring transformation, and only individual people willing to get on the altars of prayer to contend for His presence will become the kindling for God's fire.

God ignites the hearts of His people to pray, and that prayer becomes the catalyst for revival. We see this precedent in the biblical record and throughout church history—revival is preceded by sometimes years of fervent, sacrificial intercession. Prayer is what moves God's heart; it brings agreement and repentance that opens the heavens.

Just as prayer is the catalyst for revival, revival becomes the precursor for transformation. Revival is *not* the end but the beginning of a long-term process of spiritual and natural restoration of people and communities. We cannot separate these three God-purposed realities!

> JUST AS PRAYER IS THE CATALYST FOR REVIVAL, REVIVAL BECOMES THE PRECURSOR FOR TRANSFORMATION.

God's plans are so big and His power so great we just can't imagine the scope of what He has in mind in bringing salvation to people and restoration to cities. While His plans are intricate and impossible to predict, the preparation for us along the journey is fairly simple—He requires that we pray and seek His face and walk out our faith in integrity and obedience to His call. He requires that we humble ourselves, trust Him, and love people.

## INDICATORS OF TRANSFORMATION

God promises to "pour out His spirit on all flesh" (Joel 2:28). That doesn't mean just inside our church buildings! The church must become a container or "wineskin" that God can pour His glory into and a vessel through which He can release His glory. This new church structure allows the fire of revival to spread throughout the community, touching every area of life and bringing restoration. That restoration produces long-lasting fruit because believers are now mobilized to pray and minister within their sphere of influence, not just in their congregations on Sunday mornings.

How do you know that your community is on the journey toward transformation? What do we look for? Can you discern if the presence of the Lord is increasing in a community?

During the last several years of researching and documenting case studies of transformation in the world George Otis Jr. has identified ten indicators that in most cases serve as signs that transformation is occurring in a city or nation.

## TEN INDICATORS OF TRANSFORMATION:

(1) Political leaders publicly acknowledge their sin and dependence on God (2 Kings 11:17–18; 23:2; Jonah 3:6–9).

(2) New laws and business practices are put into effect (2 Chronicles 19:10; Nehemiah 10:31).

(3) The natural environment is restored to its original life-nurturing state (Leviticus 26:4–5; 2 Chronicles 7:14; Ezekiel 34:27; 36:29–30).

(4) Economic conditions improve and lead to a discernable lessening of poverty (2 Chronicles 17:3–5; Psalm 144:14; Isaiah 60:5; Amos 9:13).

(5) There is marked change in social entertainment and vices as kingdom values are integrated into the rhythm of daily life (Ezra 10:4; Nehemiah 8:10; Ecclesiastes 10:17; Acts 19:17–20).

(6) Crime and corruption diminish throughout the community (2 Kings 12:13–15; Nehemiah 5:6–12; Isaiah 60:17–18).

(7) Volunteerism increases as Christians recognize their responsibility to heal and undergird the community (Isaiah 58:10–12; 61:104).

(8) Restored hope and joy leads to a decline in divorce, bankruptcy, and suicide (Nehemiah 12:27–28, 43; Isaiah 54:11–14; 62:3, 7; Jeremiah 30:17–19; 31:11–13; Hosea 2:15).

(9) The spiritual nature of the growing socio-political renewal becomes a hot topic in the secular media (2 Chronicles 20:29; Nehemiah 6:16; Isaiah 55:5; Ezekiel 36:36; Acts 19:17).

(10) Overwhelmed by the goodness of God, grateful Christians take the embers of revival into surrounding communities and nations (2 Chronicles 17:9; Isaiah 61:6; Acts 11:20–26).[1]

As you can see, the above list is very specific and holistic. The transformation of a community occurs when the change that God brings is pervasive restoration across all arenas of community life. It doesn't mean that the community becomes perfect, but that the change is real, long-lasting, and pervasive. God wants to bring healing and justice to every sphere of society. He wants to influence the business world and the marketplace, the educational systems, arts and entertainment, congregational life, families, and the political arena.

That means that wherever you live, work, socialize, or buy your groceries, God desires to introduce His Son through you! He wants the good news of the gospel of the kingdom to fill every sphere of your community. As a carrier of God's life and glory, you can introduce kingdom principles to those you have influence with; you can demonstrate the love of Jesus to the clerk at the gas station; you can pray for healing for a co-worker; you can bless the politician and pray for his salvation.

We typically consider plans for what the Lord wants to do in our congregations, and we have such a limited perspective of the magnitude of the change God longs to bring to our communities! What would transforming revival look like in your city? During the Welsh Revival God's kingdom radically impacted communities:

> The bars were not the only places to be emptied, dance halls, theaters, and football matches all saw a dramatic decline in attendance. The courts and jails were deserted and the police found themselves without any work to do. The story is told of policemen who closed their station and formed a choir to sing at the revival meetings. Long-standing debts were repaid, church and family feuds were healed and a new unity of purpose was felt across the denominational divides.[2]

Think about the above testimony happening in your own community. Can you imagine nobody showing up for a popular sporting event because they were so in love with God's presence? Or what about liquor stores and casinos closing because nobody was frequenting them?

It's important that we don't use the word *transformation* to describe a change in our normal ministry activities. As many ministries are impacting segments of our communities and bearing good fruit change is happening. It is tempting to call that *transformation*. But if we do we will settle for less than the fullness of what God longs to do in our community! Rather than fitting what God is doing in the transformation of communities into our definition, let's allow God to stretch us and call us to a higher place of faith for the *fullness* of His purposes—according to His Word.

## Are We Ready for Transformation?

If we are going to see our cities radically transformed by the love and power of God we must move beyond program and methodology. We have to become like Jesus, be transformed into His likeness, and reach out to a lost and dying world. There are no shortcuts, no magical formulas, and no places of honor. It requires humility, dying to our own agenda, and learning how to function as the body of Christ.

Consider each thought-provoking question and ask the Lord to give you His perspective on your level of readiness for transformation in your city.

- Is the glory of God and His kingdom the focus of everything we are and do?
- Have we become desperate and hungry for the presence of Jesus in our midst?
- Do we understand our biblical identity as the bride and body of Christ?
- Are there opportunities for the citywide church to worship and pray together?
- Are we seeing our city through the eyes of the Lord?
- Are we blessing and seeking the peace of the city?
- Are we walking together in covenantal unity with the body of Christ?
- Are our hearts postured in repentance and humility?
- Have we reconciled across gender, ethnic, generational, and denominational lines?
- Have we shifted our focus from the saved to the lost?
- Is the church functioning as the priesthood in the city in spiritual power and authority?
- Is the church in the city functioning as a counterculture or merely as a subculture?

- Are we ministering to people both inside and outside the walls of the church building?
- Are we hearing God's voice corporately as we seek Him together in prayer?
- Have we restored righteousness inside the temple before we minister outside in the city?
- Are the spiritual leaders serving as "gatekeepers" of the city?
- Who is controlling the spiritual climate of the city?

## IS THERE A "MASTER KEY"?

Many methods and strategies that have been somewhat effective in other places haven't had the same impact in the Western world. We want to apply something that has been successful someplace else to our own circumstance and expect the same results. But we cannot use whatever key we want to and *hope* it opens the door to transformation, even if that particular method or principle seemed to be effective in another ministry, city, or nation. If we are applying biblical principles they will work, but if we are simply carbon-copying ministry methods, they won't. The keys may look the same, but the doors of revival and transformation won't necessarily open.

One of the fundamental differences between the non-Western world and the Western world is the level of desperation in the lives of God's people. This is a critical component in our pursuit of transformation in the West. The key of *holy desperation for the presence and ministry of Jesus* is required in order for us to move out of our complacent, satisfied existence.

Desperation is the underlying fuel that ignites our hearts for unity, prayer, worship, and repentance. If we aren't longing for Jesus our ministry activities will be routine and hollow. There is certainly no shortage of ideas, plans, methods, books, teachings, programs, and activities in the church; what we are suffering from is a drought of desperation for God!

To be desperate means to be without hope in your current condition and to know that in your own power you don't have the necessary resources required to change it. People who are desperate become determined to find help, often taking great risks to meet their desperate need. In the communities where transforming revival has occurred the people of God were desperate enough to change their lifestyle and their priorities and to commit their time and resources, making everything else a *secondary activity* to the desperate pursuit of God in their midst. They cried out in desperation, and the Lord heard their cry.

THERE IS CERTAINLY NO SHORTAGE OF IDEAS, PLANS, METHODS, BOOKS, TEACHINGS, PROGRAMS, AND ACTIVITIES IN THE CHURCH; WHAT WE ARE SUFFERING FROM IS A DROUGHT OF DESPERATION FOR GOD!

In the Western world we see very little desperation. Most of us would agree that revival is a good idea, but if we don't become desperate we will never commit ourselves to pray until we see a break-through. How many places have you witnessed people contending for the restoration of God's presence with such an intensity it seemed their lives depended on it? Only holy desperation will give us the courage to break through the spiritual "veneer" that covers the church today. We must cry out like blind Bartimaeus and ignore those who would try to keep us quiet! Or be like the woman who washed the feet of Jesus in desperate love as an act of worship, even though she was ridiculed by the disciples.

The cry of desperation pierces through religious rhetoric, and the very act of crying out will awaken the human heart to seek God. Look at the world around you, watch the news, take a good look at your city—we are a people in desperate need of the manifest presence of Jesus in our midst!

## DESPERATE PEOPLE

God has ordained purposes for His church and her ministry on the earth, and He will bring everything to a grand conclusion exactly the way He has determined. It's not up for discussion or debate, and it's not dependent upon anything or anyone other than God himself. *The only question is whether we choose to enter into what God has promised.*

History-makers are always desperate people! Only desperate people are willing to sacrifice for the sake of what burns in their hearts. Until we reach the point of desperation we won't be suffi-ciently motivated to move out of our current condition. Being part of the status quo is the antithesis of being a world-changing believer. Think about the Samaritan woman at the well in John, chapter 4. Her encounter with Jesus ignited her heart, and her whole village was evangelized as a result! When desperate people encounter Jesus transformation occurs!

We must become desperate for Jesus, first in our personal lives. When we see the condition of our own hearts, and say with Jeremiah, my "heart is deceitful above all things, and desperately wicked; Who can know it?" (17:9), we will become desperate for the nature of Jesus to be formed within us. Desperation for Jesus will lead us through the "Door of Intimacy," restoring us to our first love and intimate fellowship with the Lord. We will be like the Shulamite woman in Song of Solomon 3:4, who said, "When I found the one I love, I held him and would not let him go." The Lord promises us in Jeremiah 29:13–14: "You will seek Me and find Me, when you search for Me with all your heart. I will be found by you."

Desperation isn't something that just *happens* to us or that we casually stumble onto; we must cultivate it in our lives. It's not something that can be "served up to us" on a Sunday morning! We must set our hearts in desperate pursuit of God. The

HISTORY-MAKERS ARE ALWAYS DESPERATE PEOPLE!

Lord is inviting us to commit our hearts to Him in a new way. We must humble ourselves and prayerfully consider what changes we need to make in our lives to make room for our pursuit of God. We must open the Door of Intimacy!

Individual desperation will then lead us to corporate desperation and we will long for the presence of Jesus to fill His church! His presence among us will stir us out of our routine religion and empty entertaining activities. When we become desperate for Jesus in our midst we will see the Door of Hope open to lead us out of our wandering in the Valley of Trouble.

When the church is revived and experiencing the tangible presence of Jesus in her midst our eyes and hearts will be opened to the devastation in our communities. Then we will become desperate for the manifest presence of Jesus in our cities. That desperation and sense of spiritual responsibility will move us beyond hindrances and boundaries and into our corporate purpose as the body of Christ.

Desperation for Jesus to touch our community will open the Door of Heaven, giving us a glimpse of eternity. This in turn will unlock the transforming purpose of the church on the earth.

## BECOMING DESPERATE!

How do we become desperate for God? There are two options: We can either intentionally pursue Jesus until spiritual hunger is restored and our internal life is changed, or our external world may change unexpectedly to such a degree that we cannot go back to normal. The first option is something for which we can be responsible; the second is something over which we have no control.

The decision to make a radical lifestyle change and realign our hearts with the Lord is a matter of our will availing itself of God's grace and reprioritizing our time and commitment. We can willingly and purposefully begin to pursue God! When we do, He responds, and the more time we spend in His presence, the more desperate for Him we will become. It's an interesting dynamic; the hungrier we are for Him, the hungrier we will become for more of Him!

If our external world changes dramatically it will bring us to a place of desperation even though we certainly wouldn't choose it for ourselves. People who hesitate to open the door and move into a deeper place of intimacy with Jesus are taking a calculated risk because they assume they are in control of their own destinies. If we wait for the external motivator we will be caught off guard and our hearts, unprotected by intimacy with Jesus, could grow bitter and full of fear. Then, when the church needs to be prepared to be a place of refuge for the city, she will be dealing with her own fear and insecurity, unable to minister effectively.

How we respond at a heart level now, when Jesus is knocking at the door, is critical to how prepared we will be when things change externally around us—which eventually will be the case.

Many people are paralyzed in their spiritual life because they don't trust God enough to follow Him through the open door before them. They may dream of living a full and exciting Christian life, but deep down they realize it will cost them something and they just aren't sure they are willing to pay the price. That's how we get stuck in our religious routines and live life filled with regrets.

An intriguing question was considered by the four lepers who sat at the gate of the city, in 2 Kings 7:3. After assessing their desperate situation, one asked, "Why are we sitting here until we die?" We could ask ourselves the same question!

## WILL YOU OPEN THE DOOR?

If we are desperate for the presence of Jesus and sufficiently convinced that apart from Him we can do nothing then we must answer the knock at the door and accept His invitation!

Will you open the door? Will you follow the Lord into deeper levels of spiritual intimacy and fellowship? Are you longing to be delivered from compromise and complacency and restored to covenant and hope? Have you glimpsed God's eternal perspective through the door of heaven and do you understand your transforming purpose?

God is looking for partnership in His covenant purposes. Sometimes the invitation the Lord extends to us is terrifying, many times requiring a leap of faith or sacrifice that can be very challenging. With His invitation also comes a new level of responsibility. Stepping into a higher place of faith and adventure with God is costly; it will require more of us. We must set our hearts to be like David, who said he wouldn't offer God a sacrifice that cost him nothing (2 Samuel 24:24).

God is unpredictable! The truth is, you have no idea what He has in store for you when you accept the invitation. The greatest adventures of my life have been those times when I have answered the Lord's knock at the door. The first couple of times I did so with uncertainty because I had no idea what to expect. New steps of faith have never been easy for me, but they have always resulted in life-changing experiences with God! Now when I sense the Lord is knocking at the door, inviting me to deeper levels of faith and obedience, my first response isn't hesitation—it's a longing to be with Him.

The alternative is to be like the rich man in Matthew 19:16–22 who decided the cost of serving Jesus was too great. His material possessions meant too much to him, so he turned the invitation down and walked away. When our minds are not renewed, and we are compromised in our faith, the thought of giving, serving, and sacrificing for a kingdom that is not of this world can seem ludicrous.

But when our minds are renewed our perspective changes, our vision is restored, and our hearts burn within us for His presence. Mike Bickle (IHOP) made this comment: "When our minds are renewed, what used to seem costly now seems only reasonable."

Jesus offered His life in exchange for restored relationship with us. How can we offer Him anything less than ours?

God has more for us than we have even imagined! Paul says in 1 Corinthians 2:9: "Eye has not seen, nor ear heard, nor have entered into the heart of man the things which God has prepared for those who love Him." In our covenant relationship with God, the only thing we bring to the partnership is our love and devotion; God brings everything else! To walk through the doors before us, the doors of intimacy, hope, and heaven, and to respond to His generous invitation, we need only one master key: the key of holy desperation.

Are you *desperate for His presence*? Then open the door . . .

Lift up your heads, O you gates!
Lift up, you everlasting doors!
And the King of glory shall come in.
Who is this King of glory?
The Lord of hosts,
He *is* the King of glory.
Psalm 24:9–10

## Introduction

1. Barna Research Group, "The Year's Most Intriguing Findings, From Barna Research Studies," *Barna Research Online,* December 17, 2001. *www.barna.org/FlexPage.aspx?Page=BarnaUpdate&BarnaUpdateID=103.*

2. Barna Research Group, "Annual Study Reveals America is Spiritually Stagnant," *Barna Research Online,* March 5, 2001. *www.barna.org/FlexPage.aspx?Page=BarnaUpdate&BarnaUpdateID=84.*

## Chapter One

1. Barna Research Group, "Annual Study Reveals America is Spiritually Stagnant," *Barna Research Online,* March 5, 2001. *www.barna.org/FlexPage.aspx?Page=BarnaUpdate&BarnaUpdateID=84.*

2. Wesley Adams, *The Fire of God's Presence* (Kansas City, Mo.: Ambassadors Press, 2003), 13.

3. Ibid., 73–74.

4. To order these videos, see The Sentinel Group Web site: *www.sentinelgroup.org/videos.asp.*

5. *The Quickening,* film by The Sentinel Group. To order, see The Sentinel Group Web site: *www.sentinelgroup.org/videos.asp.*

## Chapter Two

1. Tommy Tenney, *God's Favorite House* (Shippensburg, Pa.: Destiny Image Publishers, 1999), 101.

2. A. W. Tozer, *The Pursuit of God* (Camp Hill, Pennsylvania: Christian Publishers, 1993), 17.

3. Larry Keefauver, "His Presence: The Key to Church Growth," *Ministries Today* (September/October 2002), 51–52.

4. Guido Kuwas, "The Azusa Street Revival Part II," *Global Revival News.* *www.sendrevival.com/history/azusa_street/leaders_of_azusa_street_2.htm.*

5. Wesley Duewel, *Revival Fire* (Grand Rapids, Mich.: Zondervan, 1995), 11.

6. Tozer, 35.

## Chapter Three

1. Tozer, *The Pursuit of God,* 32.

2. Tenney, *God's Favorite House,* 18.

3. Mike Bickle, *The Pleasures of Loving God* (Lake Mary, Fl.: Charisma House, 2000), 57.

*Chapter Four*

1. John Dawson, *Taking Our Cities for God* (Lake Mary, Fl.: Charisma House, 2001) 29–30.
2. Ibid., 29.
3. George Otis Jr., *Informed Intercession* (Ventura, Calif.: Renew, 1999), 21.

*Chapter Five*

1. George Barna, *The State of the Church: 2002* (Ventura, Calif.: Issachar Resources, 2002), 63.
2. Ibid., 34.
3. Thomas Owens Mackubin, "Eternally Out of Date?" *National Review Online,* September 3, 2003. *www.nationalreview.com/owens/ owens090303.asp*

*Chapter Six*

1. Oz Guiness, *Prophetic Untimeliness* (Grand Rapids, Mich.: Baker Books, 2003), 71.
2. George Barna, *The State of the Church: 2002,* 93.
3. Barna Research Group, "Annual Study Reveals America Is Spiritually Stagnant," *Barna Research Online,* March 5, 2001. *www.barna.org/ FlexPage.aspx?Page=BarnaUpdate&BarnaUpdateID=84.*
4. George Barna, *The State of the Church: 2002,* 47.
5. Ibid., 59.
6. Ibid., 69.
7. Barna Research Group, "The Year's Most Intriguing Findings," *Barna Research Online,* December 17, 2001. *www.barna.org/ FlexPage.aspx?Page=BarnaUpdate&BarnaUpdateID=103.*
8. Barna Research Group, "Researcher Predicts Mounting Challenges to Christian Church," *Barna Research Online,* April 16, 2001. *www.barna.org/FlexPage.aspx?Page=BarnaUpdate&BarnaUpdateID=88.*
9. Barna Research Group, "Spiritual Progress Hard to Find in 2003," *Barna Research Online,* December 22, 2003. *www.barna.org/ FlexPage.aspx?Page=BarnaUpdate&BarnaUpdateID=155.*
10. P. L. Tan, *Encyclopedia of 7700 Illustrations: [A treasury of illustrations, anecdotes, facts, and quotations for pastors, teachers, and Christian workers]* (Garland, Tex.: Bible Communications, 1996).
11. S. J. Hill, *Enjoying God* (Lake Mary, Fl.: Relevant Books, 2001), 37.

*Chapter Seven*

1. Barna Research Group, "Barna Identifies Seven Paradoxes Regarding America's Faith," *Barna Research Online,* December 17, 2002. *www.barna.org/FlexPage.aspx?Page=BarnaUpdate&BarnaUpdateID=128.*
2. Tenney, *God's Favorite House,* 67.
3. George Otis Jr., unpublished teaching notes.

4. To order, see The Sentinel Group Web site: *www.sentinelgroup.org/ videos.asp*.
5. "The Welsh Revival of 1904: Evan Roberts," *The Watchword,* vol. 25. *www.sendrevival.com/history/welsh_revival/evan_roberts_brief.htm*.

## Chapter Nine

1. Ames Garlow, *The Covenant* (Kansas City, Mo.: Beacon Hill Press of Kansas City, 1999), 17–21.
2. Ibid., 50.

## Chapter Ten

1. Tozer, *The Pursuit of God,* 18.

## Chapter Eleven

1. Promise Keepers Web site: *www.promisekeepers.org/core/core10.htm*.

## Chapter Twelve

1. *Let the Seas Resound*. Film by The Sentinel Group, 2004.
2. Julian Watts, Re: "Guildford" Email to Author, February 22, 2004.
3. Tozer, *The Pursuit of God,* 18.

## Chapter Thirteen

1. James Orr, general editor, *International Standard Bible Encyclopedia,* vol. 2, (Grand Rapids, Mich.: Eerdmans Publishing Co., 1978), 762–63.
2. Ibid.

## Chapter Fourteen

1. George Otis Jr., unpublished teaching notes.
2. Robert L. Bradshaw, "Bending the Church to Save the World: The Welsh Revival of 1904" (1995). *www.sendrevival.com/history/welsh_ revival/bending_save_the_world_bradshaw.htm*.

# About Fusion Ministries

Fusion Ministries, Inc. is a ministry dedicated to the pursuit of God's presence and glory becoming a tangible reality in both individual lives and entire communities. We serve as a catalyst to ignite fire for revival and hope for transformation of communities, cities and nations.

The primary emphasis of the ministry is to provide inspiration, consultation and teaching key principles from God's Word to encourage the citywide church to prepare for the habitation of God's presence.

Fusion Ministries is called to serve as a "bridge" to connect three important realities of the Kingdom: the call to intimacy with Jesus, the vision of transforming revival, and the mandate to take that message to the nations.

If you would like additional information about our ministry or are interested in becoming involved in revival and transformation activities please contact us:

Fusion Ministries, Inc.

P.O. Box 480255
Kansas City, MO 64148

Telephone: (816) 965-5470

*www.Fusionministry.com*